NECESSITIES

RACIAL
BARRIERS
IN AMERICAN
SPORTS

NECESSITIES

PHILLIP M.
HOOSE

RANDOM HOUSE
NEW YORK

Library of Congress Cataloging-in-Publication Data
Hoose, Phillip M.
    Necessities: racial barriers in American sports.
    1. Discrimination in sports—United States.
2. Afro-American athletes—Social conditions. I. Title.
GV706.32.H66 1989 305.8'08996073 88-43227
ISBN 0-394-56944-X

Book design by Debbie Glasserman

Manufactured in the United States of America
98765432
First Edition

TO THE CLEVELAND BARRACUDAS

ACKNOWLEDGMENTS

The idea for this book was available to any writer who takes an interest in sports, but I'd like to thank my editor, Erroll McDonald, for encouraging me to address it and helping me define it. Thanks also to my agent, Philip Spitzer, for his consistent encouragement and friendship. Many thanks to Patti Williams for typing transcripts and calling often, and to Tim, Darwin, and Peggy Hoose for their support. My greatest appreciation is to Shoshana and Hannah Hoose.

Thanks to Alan Reinhardt and Jon Halvorsen for reviewing chapter drafts, and to Eileen O'Brien, Buck Briggs, Chris Nesbitt, Roland Guinzberg, Buck Dawson, Tom Sanders, Epy Guerrero, Abel Alvarez, Terrie Williams, Kenneth Shropshire, Julio Reyes, Tom Heitz, Wayne Patterson, Patricia Kelly, and Dr. Richard Lapchik for opening doors, offering ideas and insights, translating from Spanish, and providing reference material.

I also wish to thank, for perspective, and for assisting with the location of photographs and reference material, staff members of the National Black Media Coalition, Northeastern University's Center for the Study of Sport in Society, the National Baseball, Basketball, and Football Halls of Fame, and the International Swimming Hall of Fame, the Cleveland Barracudas Swim Club, the National Football League Players Association, the Savannah Cardinals baseball club, and the United States Swimming Office. Thanks also to Black Cow Photo for providing print reproductions.

Last but by no means least, I wish to thank the following athletes, family members, coaches, scouts, agents, administrators, broadcasters, agents, entrepreneurs, journalists, and officials who kindly allowed me to interview them: Tracy Lewis, W. W. Law, William Pleasant, William Ackerman, Julius Fine, Mike Blaser, Robert James, Donald Heath, Dr. Robert E. Lee, Moby McLeod, Phyllis, Cartrina, Sandra, and Warren Moore, Denise, Charon, and Candra Jolly, Roberto Cottingham, Josie Mais, Byron Davis, Barbara Davis, Jerry Holtrey, Dr. John Troup, Jeff Diamond, Ed Reed, Chris Silva, Dessie Silva, Eldon Alexander, Keith Lee, Sandy Stephens, Willie Thrower, Joe Gilliam, Tony Dungy, Leo Cahill, David Watkins, Dwight Stephenson, Earl Battey, Elrod Hendricks, Larry Doby, Sam Hairston, Shirley Povich, Sam Lacey, Jack Schwarz, Frank Genovese, Pat Gillick, Rafael Avila, Ramon Linares, Sijo Linares, Rico Carty, Rafael Ramirez, Alfredo Griffin, Gordon Ash, Juan Castro, Miguel Piri, Billy Packer, Dick Vitale, Calvin Hill, Pluria Marshall, Sonny Hill, Harold Bell, Ed Jones, Larry Whiteside, Joe Butler, Tom Conchawski, Rick Ball, Haskell Cohen, Guy Rodgers, John Grunkmeyer, Maurice LaMar, Sam Drummer, Sherman Douglas, Wayne Morgan, Darryl Orlando Ledbetter, Fred Slaughter, Jane Stafford, and Donn Clendenon.

CONTENTS

On the Monday evening of April 6, 1987, Al Campanis, who, although he had no way of knowing it, would be for only two more days vice-president for player personnel for the Los Angeles Dodgers, wired up in the Houston Astrodome to take questions from Ted Koppel, the host of ABC's *Nightline.* The occasion for Campanis's appearance was the fortieth anniversary of the day that Jackie Robinson became the first black man to play in a major league game. On that day, Robinson was wearing a Dodger uniform while Campanis, four years after his retirement as a player, was starting an administrative career with the Dodgers that would span nearly a half-century. *Nightline*'s staff pursued Al Campanis because he was the only person who had been both a firsthand witness to baseball's integration and a major player in the personnel decisions of its aftermath.

For Campanis, it had already been a lousy night. Just a few

hours before, the Dodgers had blown their opening game of the season, losing to the Houston Astros on a late-inning, two-run homer. As the camera lights came on Campanis appeared on the screen as a jowly man with thinning black hair, dressed in a Dodger-blue coat, shirt, and tie. His head tilted to one side, with the Astrodome's synthetic turf in the background, he began to field Koppel's questions. He looked like he was having trouble with his earphone.

Koppel began by leading Campanis and author Roger Kahn through the life and times of Jackie Robinson and then, after two or three minutes, he shifted gears abruptly. He asked Campanis, "Why are there no black managers, general managers, or owners? . . . Is there still that much prejudice in baseball today?"

"No," Campanis answered, "I don't believe it's prejudice. I truly believe they may not have some of the necessities to be, let's say, a field manager or perhaps a general manager." The remark gave rise to the following exchange:

KOPPEL: Do you really believe that?

CAMPANIS: Well, I don't say that all of them, but they certainly are short. How many quarterbacks do you have, how many pitchers do you have that are black?

KOPPEL: Yeah, but I got to tell you, that sounds like the same garbage we were hearing forty years ago about players.

CAMPANIS: No, it's not garbage, Mr. Koppel, because I played on a college team, and the center fielder was black, and in the backfield at NYU was a fullback who was black. Never knew the difference whether he was black or white. We were teammates. So it might just be, why are black men or black people not good swimmers? Because they don't have the buoyancy.

They took a break. The ABC switchboards flooded with calls. When they came back, Koppel offered Campanis a chance to "dig yourself out," but Campanis instead dug himself in deeper, suggesting that blacks "may not have the desire to be in the front office." "They're outstanding athletes," he added, "very God-gifted, and they're wonderful people . . . They are gifted with great musculature and various other things. They're fleet of foot. And this is why there are a lot of black major league ballplayers. Now as far as having the background to become club presidents or presidents of a bank . . . I don't know."

It was a remarkable exchange. Campanis's observations amounted to an intact record of the semiconscious values of those who control major sports in America. It was all there—the residue of decades of dugout talk, winter meetings, road meals, hotel lobbies, scouting reports, and banquets.

Campanis's statements laid it all bare for examination: Blacks can't think. They have no ambition. Can't float. Don't know how to lead. They have great bodies. They are, as a race, gifted physically but deficient mentally. It all boiled down to the one word "necessities." Blacks lacked, in his view, some basic equipment, some complement of traits possessed by those who control sports, on or off the field. This book, more than about the sports or the athletes themselves, is about the "necessities."

■

Blacks make up about 12 percent of the American population. Black median income is, according to a report by the National Urban League, only 57 percent that of whites. The black poverty rate in 1986 was nearly three times that of whites. The rate of unemployment for black youth is nearly double that of white youth. Yet, black players make up 77 percent of all NBA players and 62 percent of all NFL starters. Some of these athletes earn millions of dollars each year, and many signed for huge bonuses. On the face of it, sports would seem to be a model for racial progress. But, although appearances may have changed, four decades after Jackie Robinson's major league debut, racial prejudice remains as deeply rooted in American sports as it is in American society in general.

■

"[Jackie] Robinson will not make the grade in major league baseball," predicted Jimmy Powers, sports editor of the New York *Daily News*. "He is a thousand-to-one shot at best. The Negro players simply don't have the brains or skills."

Forty years later, by the words and images they choose, broadcasters and writers continue to convey racial stereotypes—portraying blacks as undisciplined brutes, Latins as explosive little firecrackers, and whites as heady, gutty leaders who overcome their damned inferior equipment through Puritan effort. Blacks are described in terms of hang time, are encouraged to say "hi, Mom" after touchdowns, are said to make mental mistakes and to have innate "athletic ability."

Whites are said to be born with "white man's disease"—they can't run or jump—but continue to hustle and scrap anyway, filling the passing lanes, anticipating well, and digging for superior position. "When [Larry] Bird makes a great play," said Isiah Thomas, "it's due to his thinking and work habits. It's all planned out for him. It's not the case for blacks. All we do is run and jump. We never practice or give a thought to how we play. It's like I came dribbling out of my mother's womb."

While watching a game, any baseball or football fan can easily see racial stereotypes at work. A scorecard and these two principles will help:

1. The nearer that a position is to where the ball usually is, the less likely it is that a black will occupy it.
2. The more responsibility or control involved in a position, the less likely it is that a black will play it.

Rather than try a black player out at quarterback or catcher, coaches will stockpile them as defensive backs, wide receivers, and outfielders. They will say they are doing this to avoid squandering black running speed in positions that don't require great mobility. Instead they end up wasting the tactical ability and leadership potential of people who happen to have dark skin.

The 1988 major league baseball All-Star game provides a good case in point. Nine of the eleven outfielders, players who wait for five or six chances a game to run after a struck ball, were black or Latin. Fourteen of the twenty-three infielders, including all the American League starters, were white. All four catchers, the strategists who decide which pitch will be thrown, were white (there hasn't been a American-born black starting catcher in major league baseball since 1980, and only two since 1970). Nineteen of the twenty pitchers—the players who initiate action and control the pace of the game—were white, with Dwight Gooden the only exception. Black baseball players are today nearly nine times as likely to be outfielders as pitchers; about four of five blacks who play defensive positions are either outfielders or first basemen. Only about 40 percent of all whites play those positions.

Off the field, almost all the blacks who have ever been hired as baseball coaches have been hitting instructors or have coached first base—where you get to slap singles hitters on the butt and remind them how many outs there are. In 1987 the only minority third-base coach—the person who relays the manager's wishes to hitters and makes decisions about trying to score runs—was Ozzie Virgil, a Hispanic.

The NFL's biases are, if possible, even more graphic. According to a survey commissioned by *The Boston Globe,* on the last day of the 1987–88 NFL season, 62 percent of all players in the twenty-eight starting lineups were black. But a black was almost 50 percent more likely to be playing defense, reacting to someone else's plan, than offense, starting the action. Linebackers—the control centers of the defense—were almost twice as likely to be whites as players at any other defensive position.

On offense, the planning positions—the quarterback, who directs the play, and the center, who initiates it by snapping the ball—were almost entirely filled by whites. All of the fifty-six kickers but one—Miami's Reggie Roby, perhaps the best punter in the league—were white. Most offensive linemen were white. "They're the real thinkers of the team," L.A. Rams coach John Robinson once explained to *Sports Illustrated* writer Paul Zimmerman. "The receivers [93 percent black in the *Globe* survey] just say, 'Throw me the ball.' The runners [89 percent black] say, 'Hand me the ball.' But offensive linemen stop and say, 'Why are we doing that?' "

The farther an offensive lineman was from the ball, the more likely he was to be black: Seven percent of all centers, 23 percent of guards, and 46 percent of tackles were black. There have been only a handful of black centers in the history of the NFL (only three between 1960 and 1979, according to a survey conducted by the NFL Players Association) and only two black starting centers in 1987. Both of them—the Colts' Ray Donaldson and Miami's Dwight Stephenshon—were All-Pro.

The center makes more decisions and has greater latitude than anyone on the field but the quarterback. "I'm right there in the middle," says Stephenson. "The left tackle can't see what's going on in front of the right tackle. So I have the best position, other than the quarterback, to see what's happening. The center has to decide whether to use the blocking pattern we decided in the huddle or, if the defense gives us a different look, to go with a different blocking scheme. I can change it with an audible at the line of scrimmage."

Does racial prejudice account for the scarcity of black centers? "No one's ever made a racial remark," says Stephenson. "But you can look around and see that there's not a lot of black centers, just like you don't see a lot of black quarterbacks. I think now we're showing we can play the position as well as anybody. They'll have to play the best person if they want to win."

Blacks are rarely in a position to control the ball or the field of play because they are even more rarely in a position to manage the game off the field. There has never, for instance, in the history of the NFL, been a black head coach, and there has been only one black coordinator of an offensive or defensive unit. In 1983, when the New Orleans Saints' head coaching job surfaced, Elijah Pitts, fifty, an ex–NFL running back who had the longest tenure of any black assistant coach in the NFL—twelve years—wrote a letter of application. His hopes weren't soaring, but then, nothing happens unless you try. His letter was never even acknowledged. "It was quite discouraging and I haven't applied since," he told the Cleveland *Plain Dealer* in 1987. "That's what happens to a lot of guys."

In baseball, there is a small group of white managers who have held more managing jobs than all blacks combined in the history of the game. If Jackie Robinson were alive today, one person he would recognize on the sporting scene would be his old Dodger teammate Don Zimmer. Zimmer, at this writing the manager of the Chicago Cubs, is a charter member of an exclusive club of baseball men who pass through dugout after dugout, front office after front office, men whose names crop up—because, it is said, they are experienced—whenever management vacancies appear. Zimmer, whose lifetime winning percentage entering the 1988 season was .508, beat out the other two candidates for the Cubs job—Billy Williams, a black, and Pat Corrales, a Hispanic—in a time-honored way: He knew somebody.

Zimmer had previously worked for his employer, Cubs general manager Jim Frey, as a third-base coach. As it turns out, he used to double-date with Dallas Green, who had hired him in a previous job. (In fact, at present, three National League managers—Atlanta's Russ Nixon, Chicago's Zimmer, and Cincinnati's Pete Rose—went to the same Cincinnati high school, from which Frey is also a graduate.) Really, it was no contest; Don Zimmer's managerial experience shone through his every gesture: He looked like a manager, acted like a manager, chewed and spat like a manager, hunkered in the dugout like a manager, and thought like a manager. It didn't matter that he had won barely half his games in a prolonged managerial career—one candidate was Zim, and the other two weren't. It was as simple as that.

In February 1989, Bill White, a black ex–first baseman and longtime broadcaster, was named to replace A. Bartlett Giamatti as president of the National League.

It was a strong statement and a positive beginning, but major league baseball's work is hardly finished. White's job is largely that of a disciplinarian, ruling on fines and suspensions of players, settling disputes between managers and umpires. Authentic power rests with the twenty-six team owners and their general managers, key executives, and field managers—almost all of whom are white.

"Name baseball's 100 most powerful people—owners, league executives and general managers—and 99 are white males," wrote *Washington Post* sportswriter Tom Boswell in a 1988 column about why baseball hasn't returned to Washington, D.C. "Many are conservative, a few reactionary. Al Campanis was typical." It is no wonder that more than a century after the first professional sports team was established no black has ever owned a major league American franchise in any sport. From time to time blacks have tried to get a piece of the pie, but always the door has been closed.

Those who own teams, stadiums, and sports arenas control what has been estimated to be about five thousand off-the-field jobs. Even in the NBA, many of whose staff employees are black and where a handful of executives wield the only traces of authentic black power on the American sporting scene, very little of the net economic output of a game or a season—the real pie to be sliced up—is controlled by blacks.

The 1988 NBA All-Star game had the demographic profile of the first Kentucky Derby. Fourteen of the first fifteen jockeys in the first Derby, run in 1875, were black, ex-slaves or sons of freedmen. Likewise, all the entertainers on both All-Star teams, with the exception of three white Boston Celtics—were black. Though many of the players were millionaires, in some ways the similarities between the All-Star game and the first Derby were more profound than the differences.

Most fans who could afford tickets were white. All the referees were white. All the broadcasters, with the exception of CBS's James Brown, who was stationed in the locker room, were white, as were the programs' producers and directors and all but one of CBS Sports's senior executives. All the league's team owners, all but two general managers and four head coaches were white. It is safe to say that virtually everyone who made any serious money off the game besides the players, from those who controlled the point spread to the key executives and shareholders of the companies that bought TV time, to the printers of programs and tickets, mammoth waste-management companies that generally haul away trash from major sporting events, agents and attorneys, parking concessionaires, vendors, were white.

There are different ways to look at black players' growing domination of sports like basketball and football. "Well, they've [blacks] got everything," complained then–CBS broadcaster Jimmy "the Greek" Snyder in a D.C. restaurant one night three weeks before the NBA All-Star game. "If they take over coaching like everybody wants them to, there's not going to be anything left for white people." D.C. radio sports commentator Harold Bell, a black ex–wide receiver who for fifteen years has been trying to crack the white world of sports broadcasting, sees it another way. As it did for Snyder, the NBA All-Star game carried Bell's thoughts back to plantation days. Sports, Bell remarked, was one of the few professions where employees were still controlled by people called "owners."

Bell observed that black boxers and jockeys were the first American professional athletes. In the late eighteenth century, southern cotton planters, having come in contact with boxing in Great Britain, organized high-stakes boxing matches and horse races matching slave against slave. The boxers lived in cabins with comfortable beds, and were fed better than the field hands or domestics. Some even had slaves of their own. They were, in the words of sports journalist and historian Wells Twombly, "valuable housepets."

Boxers and jockeys wore the plantation's colors when they competed. The stakes were enormous, and in some ways little different than they are now: The boxer who could make his master a rich man could win his freedom. The terms were very clear, and often recorded in local courthouses as contracts; to become a free man the boxer had to win either a certain number of matches or a certain amount of money for his master. "Symbolically, it hasn't changed much, has it?" Bell asked a companion. "We can still do all the labor but we can't make decisions or profits."

■

This book is not a history of the black athlete. Rather, it is a guide to the racial biases and racially influenced practices operating in American sports today. It explores the "necessities" for black sportsmen and sportswomen who want to control their destiny on or off the field. It is based largely on about one hundred interviews with coaches, team executives, scouts, athletes and their family members, agents, journalists, academics, and broadcasters conducted throughout the United States and the Dominican Republic in 1987 and the first half of 1988.

The book addresses such questions as: Why, in their four-game coverage of Indiana University's road to the 1987 NCAA basketball championship, did CBS announcers Brent Musburger and Billy Packer use the words "athlete" or "athletic" to describe blacks, while almost all references to thought or discipline were applied to whites? Is money irrelevant to the prospect of blacks ever owning a major sports franchise? Why have only eight black quarterbacks thrown more than twenty-five passes in the history of the National Football League? Why, three quarters of a century after the first black Olympic dashman, have there been no black U.S. Olympic swimmers? Why is the U.S. Labor Department, with the acquiescence of major league baseball, regulating the number of foreign-born professional players—almost all of them dark-skinned Latins? Why are there so few black pitchers? Why has there been no starting American-born black catcher in major league baseball since 1980? Why must those who are paid by college basketball recruiters to prepare scouting reports on high school players publish each player's race?

Sports has long been hailed as the great racial leveler, the opportunity for athletes and spectators of all races to mingle on common ground. But since Jackie Robinson took the field on that April day in 1947, the thousands of games that the descendants of slaves and slave owners have played in public together have not served to bring us appreciably closer.

At the beginning, some fans were able to deny that races were actually mixing on our playing fields. From Jackie Robinson's day to the early sixties, for instance, the companies that produced baseball, football, and basketball cards often drew pictures of blacks as whites with burr haircuts, as in the depiction of Frank Robinson and Bill Russell on Robinson's 1959 baseball card below:

FRANK ROBINSON

285

A mysterious arm ailment has plagued Frank off and on for the past few years. Birdie Tebbetts has used him at first base in such instances. But it hasn't affected Frank's terrific homer total since coming up from Columbia.

FRESHMAN FUN!

FRANK WAS A HIGH SCHOOL TEAMMATE OF BASKETBALL STAR BILL RUSSELL

HE TIED A RECORD FOR FIRST-YEAR MEN BY BELTING 38 HOMERS IN '56

Height: 6'1"
Weight: 185
Bats: Right
Throws: Right
Home: Oakland, Cal.
Born: Aug. 31, 1935

MAJOR LEAGUE BATTING RECORD									FIELDING			
	Games	AB	Runs	Hits	2B	3B	HR	RBI	B.Avg	PO	A	E	F.Avg
YEAR	150	611	97	197	29	5	29	75	.322	487	36	6	.989
LIFE	302	1183	219	363	56	11	67	158	.307	810	41	14	.984

But now, thirty years after the last white heavyweight champion, at a time when several major sports are dominated statistically and numerically by people with dark skin, denial has given way to a hard-crusted estrangement. No account of modern racial relations in sports is more poignant or telling than Bill Russell's retrospective on his first twenty years in the NBA: "As a rookie," he wrote in his autobiography *Second Wind*, "I was the only black player on the Boston Celtics, and I was excluded from almost everything except practices and the games. Exactly twenty years later I was coach and general manager of the Seattle Super-Sonics, which had only two *white* players on the team—and they were excluded from almost everything but practice and the games. I told the blacks how unfair this was, and they made a token effort to change, but they said white players were just too different."

■

When Al Campanis lost his head on a bad day, he opened a heavy closet door. Here is a look inside.

NECESSITIES

THE MEDIA:

THOROUGHBREDS

AND SCRAPPERS

"People talk about my great eyesight and reflexes as if those were the reasons for my success. That's bullshit. Do you know how I learned to hit a ball? Practice, dammit. Practice, practice, practice, practice! Trial and error, trial and error, trial and error!"
—BASEBALL IMMORTAL TED WILLIAMS ON HIMSELF

"He's a great athlete. He moves well and can run. And those things come from heaven. You don't have to develop it, because it's there."
—TED WILLIAMS ON BLACK CINCINNATI OUTFIELDER ERIC DAVIS

There was a time when professional basketball was dominated by Jews. During the late thirties and early forties, when scoring machines and playmakers had names like Holzman and Passon and Holman and Borgmann, the sporting press sought and advanced genetic explanations for Jewish dominance. "Jewish players seem to take naturally to the game," wrote columnist Ed Sullivan, the man who later brought Señor Wences, Elvis, and the Beatles into your homes. "Perhaps this is because the Jew is a natural gambler and will take chances. Perhaps it is because he devotes himself more closely to a problem than others will. Whatever the reason, the fact remains that some of the greatest stars of today are Jewish players."

Many Jews moved up and out of the tough neighborhoods that have always produced great basketball players, and the game was taken over by Irish Catholics, who were said to succeed because they were innately combative. The black athletes who today make up most of the NBA and NFL labor forces, and who have begun to penetrate country-club and even Nordic sports, have heard their success explained in terms of their hands, tendons, muscles, joints, nerves, blood, thighs, African ancestry (you had to be quick and springy there), and even eye color. But not their minds. We search Larry Bird's game—not Magic Johnson's—for signs of genius. Magic is just magic.

"A stereotype," wrote Dr. Gordon Allport in his classic work of social psychology *The Nature of Prejudice,* "is an exaggerated belief associated with a category. Its function is to justify, or rationalize, our conduct in relation to that category." Whites' conduct in relation to the category "black athletes" has been to demean them by rendering them subhuman; they don't succeed by virtue of human attributes, like thought, planning, or control. They just react.

The genetic explanations for black athletic superiority have varied widely in the past half-century, but the quest for such explanations—and the reason for the pursuit—has remained constant as the North Star. The Black Natural Athlete has arisen to ease the pain of lost turf. It has not been easy for whites to see Jim Brown displace Red Grange or to see basketball swept away almost entirely by blacks or to witness the steady encroachment of black and Latin stars on the national pastime or to have to yearn for a Great White Hope in boxing. Setbacks are easier to take if it is possible to believe they are inevitable.

The same phenomenon occurs when turf is threatened in any field. Children of Southeast Asian descent, for instance, whose spectacular academic achievements have threatened notions of white academic superiority, have seen their efforts described in racial terms and have compared their plight to that of the black athlete: "All of us are proud of our ethnicity," wrote eleven Asian science students in a 1988 letter to *The New York Times*, "but we are concerned that whenever a group of people such as ours is given wide attention and scrutiny, there is a danger of losing the individuality of each person in that group. Such labeling leads to stereotyping, which in its most extreme form is the root of prejudice, a disease that can never be cured by science. The issue should not be taken too lightly, especially following the reaction to recent statements made by Jimmy (the Greek) Snyder toward another minority group, also the victim of racism."

The myth of the Black Natural Athlete—that marvelously relaxed individual of African ancestry whose jungle-honed speed and power were genetically promoted by American cotton planters—became prevalent when Jesse Owens, Ralph Metcalfe, Eddie Tolan, Eulace Peacock, and Mack Robinson, among others, began to outsprint whites in the mid-1930s. At the time, track and field was the door open widest to blacks, and the Olympic Games the only available showcase. Blacks were barred from competing for the heavyweight boxing championship between 1915, when whites finally pried it loose from Jack Johnson, and 1937 (several states actually passed laws with stiff fines barring interracial fights). At the time, major league team sports remained open to whites only. Even though Negro League baseball players did well against their white counterparts, and the all-black New York Rens may have been the world's best basketball team, interracial contests were viewed as exhibitions, divertissements that left no mark on the collective white ego. At the racetrack, blacks were back in the stables after nearly two centuries' experience as jockeys. Black swimmers were all but unknown, and the only blacks around golf courses were caddies.

Black Olympians put the writing on the wall. Until 1932, only two black athletes—both successful broad jumpers, had worn the red, white, and blue at the games, but in 1932, eighteen black athletes made the final Olympic trials at Stanford and four made the team. In 1936, nine black runners and jumpers came home with medals, sweeping all running events up to eight hundred meters, and both the long and high jumps.

After the 1936 games, the air became thick with genetic explanations for the blacks' success. Dean Cromwell, a white track coach from the University of Southern California who coached the sprint relay teams in the 1936 Olympic Games, later wrote that blacks excelled because they were "closer to the primitive." "It was not so long ago that his ability to run and jump was a life-and-death matter to him in the jungle," wrote Cromwell. "His muscles are pliable, and his easygoing disposition is a valuable aid to the mental and physical relaxation that a runner and jumper must have."

When black boxers began routinely to take titles away from whites, it was said that they were champions because their primitive nervous systems rendered them less sensitive to pain. Also black fighters were said to benefit from thicker skulls.

It's impossible to say how many whites have received their formative images of blacks by watching the Harlem Globetrotters, once a good basketball team that, starting in the 1940s, became the most popular sports franchise in world history by presenting black males as subhumans. "The worst aspect of the Trotters," wrote David Wolf in his biography of Connie Hawkins, *Foul,* "is that they affirm in the minds of whites—particularly youngsters— the stereotype of the black man as lazy, mischievous, and mentally inferior. On the court, the ideal Globetrotter exudes no pride or self-respect. He gallops about with high-stepping strides, loosing shrill jungle sounds, clapping his hands, waving his long arms, and grinning to show his teeth. . . . He pulls sneaky tricks on the white referee, shows off his athletic prowess, calls his friends by foolish names like 'Meadowlark' and 'Goose', and gives the impression that he is a devilish adolescent, full of 'natural' talent, but in need of mature handling."

Before the major leagues were integrated, whites laughed at the notion of blacks playing baseball. King Saxon, a white columnist for the Brooklyn *Times Union,* described the opening day of the 1935 Negro National League season as if he were enjoying a day at the circus: "It is safe to say that never have so many huge, flat feet trampled the grass at Ebbets Field at one time. . . . The outfielders go after fly balls like infants chasing balloons. . . . Usually the infielders are out of position for the different hitters, indicating that they don't study the opposing batsmen and shift for them. In spite of these faults, however, they play a flashy, interesting game. There isn't one of them who can't make the easiest ball look hard in fielding it, and the rule 'two hands while you're learning' doesn't seem to apply."

In the late forties and throughout the fifties a remarkable pioneer generation of black ballplayers, men like Ernie Banks, Willie Mays, Roy Campanella, Larry Doby, and Henry Aaron, whose ambition and skill had been hardened in the Negro Leagues, made ridicule of black performance impossible. But being good didn't make them completely human, either. Trying to slip a fastball past Henry Aaron, it was said, was like trying to sneak the sun past a rooster. White pitchers swore that Aaron was actually asleep at the plate—that is, until a pitch sailed by and his amazing wrists snapped out at the ball. Ernie Banks—another wrist hitter—was simply happy. Willie Mays arrived as an exuberant naïf in a man's body, who played stickball with children in his off hours.

Everyone knew that Mickey Mantle was the brooding product of a martinet father's calculated baseball regimen, a drive to the big leagues that started when Mickey was in diapers. But we heard nothing about Mays's father, William, who, as it turns out, was very much like Mutt Mantle. Mays senior taught his son to walk at six months by beckoning him toward a baseball placed on a chair. Both fathers viewed baseball as a way for their sons to escape the hard labor of their own lives—Mantle's in an Oklahoma mine and Mays's in a Birmingham, Alabama, steel mill. While fans came to know about Ted Williams's Salvation Army mother and Joe DiMaggio's fishing family, we learned little about the lives and families of black greats such as Frank Robinson and Ernie Banks and Henry Aaron and Roberto Clemente. They arrived and departed from our lives without context, without family history, without dimension.

By the late sixties, half the NBA players were black, and black performance was overtaking white performance in several other sports as well. It was impossible to ignore. In 1971 *Sports Illustrated* published a cover story ascribing black athletic superiority to inherited, racial factors. Bill Russell, the most successful basketball player ever, reacted in anger. "I worked at basketball up to eight hours a day for twenty years—straining, learning, sweating, studying—but *Sports Illustrated* didn't mention such factors as a reason for blacks' success in sports," Russell wrote. "Or all the forces that turned my ambition to basketball instead of, say, banking. No, I was good at basketball because of my bone structure. All of which shows how far out in the twilight zone your thinking can drift if it comes from a weird starting point. All the racial upheaval of the 1960's had taught *Sports Illustrated* that it's okay to be racist as long as you try to sound like a doctor."

Ironically, blacks often have been presumed limited physiologically, until overwhelming success has inverted the presumption into a quest for innate advantages. After Jesse Owens and his Olympic teammates showed the world that blacks could run fast, it was said that they were built for speed but that they couldn't run far. Now that black African marathoners are among the best in the world, the talk has stopped. Today, a few black swimmers, such as UCLA's Chris Silva, Holland's Enith Brigitha, and Suriname's Anthony Nesty, have begun to place in international swimming meets as sprinters, and the search for limits is likewise shifting to the distances. "It's just a matter of pool time and you will see black distance swimmers in the near future," says Jeff Diamond of the U.S. Swimming office. "And role models."

■

Today, even in a society where pure racial distinctions have been blurred by many generations of interracial marriage, the image of the clownish, loose, undisciplined, but instinctive black athlete lives on. Physiologists are still probing for "fast-twitch fibers" in blacks, using stop-action photography to find clues to success in the way they walk, asking them to jump off various things to see if they bounce back up faster than whites.

But with or without supporting data—and increasingly fewer blacks seem willing to cooperate in studies whose conclusions could be used to discredit their individual accomplishments—the stereotype survives, transmitted, sometimes unintentionally, by sports broadcasters and writers, almost all of whom are white. The "native" lives in the sports media's cultivation of a high-fiving, Ickey-shuffling, hi-momming, knee-wiggling-while-spiking black entertainer, a member of the exclusive Phi Slamma Jamma fraternity. It survives in the nearly exclusive association of the word *athlete* with black people, and in the enduring notion that whites are more fit to control play.

"We are insulted on a continual basis," says Pluria Marshall, chairman of the National Black Media Coalition, a Washington-based civil rights organization that monitors programming, "by white announcers who are insensitive to the history and culture and values of the black athlete." NBC's Bryant Gumbel, who began his career as a sportscaster, agrees. "How many times do you listen to an NFL game and every black guy making a catch has blinding speed and natural talent but a guy like [the white] Steve Largent is a hard worker who runs intelligent routes?" Gumbel asked in a 1987 interview with *The Washington Post.* "Every black guy is gifted and every white guy uses his head."

A case in point is CBS's coverage of Indiana University's road to the 1987 NCAA basketball championship. The Indiana team often had three blacks and two whites on the floor, but during their four-game coverage of the Hoosiers, broadcaster Billy Packer and his partner Brent Musburger used the word "athlete" or a derivative like "athletic" to describe only the black players.

During the four games (Indiana versus Auburn, Louisiana State University, the University of Nevada–Las Vegas, and Syracuse), thirteen blacks and no whites were described as "quick" (although Indiana's Steve Eyl, who is white, once made "a quick hand move"). Blacks were described in subhuman terms far more frequently than white players: Keith Smart "exploded" repeatedly. Derrick Coleman was a "plastic man" who had "Sam Perkins [another black basketball player] arms," and a remarkable "arm-span discrepancy." Once, when LSU's Oliver Brown tipped a rebound to himself and pulled it quickly into his hands, Packer was reminded of "one of those animals that catch those flies with their tongue." Musburger observed that Indiana's Rick Calloway was "gonna be a thoroughbred." Only once was a white player an animal, when Indiana's Steve Alford, a coach's son, was described as a "gym rat."

Even though fewer whites than blacks played in the four games, and only four—Indiana's Steve Alford, Steve Eyl, and Joe Hillman and Syracuse center Rony Seikaly—played significant amounts of time, whites, according to Musburger and Packer, did almost all the thinking. Whites alone were said to have hustled, made good decisions, understood the game, distributed the ball well, been wise, listened, had concentration, played technically, thought, or played with discipline. Blacks were, however, on occasion credited with leadership ability and hard work. The only two times the word "mental" was used was when a black Auburn guard "let his mental game get away" and when Keith Smart made the "mental" mistake of fouling Freddie Banks.

A striking example of the contrast between CBS's description of whites and that of blacks occurred in the Indiana-UNLV game. Late in the second half, Packer noticed that Indiana's substitute guard Joe Hillman—who is white—had been playing for a long time in favor of starter Keith Smart—who is black. "[Smart is] the kind of a guy who would love to be challenged athletically by UNLV," explained Packer, "but that's not what [Indiana coach] Bobby Knight needs today. So he goes with a Hillman who'll play within himself."

About three minutes later, Smart reentered the game. He quickly hit a lay-up, and then, with twenty-eight seconds left, tried to strip the ball away from a UNLV player. A foul was called. Packer, an ex-coach, found in this an occasion for general instruction. "That's a foul Hillman does not make," he explained. "And although Smart has done a great job for Indiana this year, that was a mental mistake, not a physical mistake."

Several months after his descriptions of Hillman and Smart, Packer stood by them as precise technical appraisals. "Other than Joe Hillman's ability to think on a court and to do the things Bobby Knight tells him to do, Joe Hillman can't play. Where can Joe Hillman play? Who can Joe Hillman play for? If he were black I'd say the same thing." Packer attributes Smart's success to a high school growth spurt. "If he were still five eight he wouldn't be playing," Packer said. "Now everybody wants him. Why? Because he's a great athlete now and he wasn't then."

Broadcasters react defensively to the notion that they perpetuate racial stereotypes. CBS's Tommy Heinsohn, stung by pro-basketball star Isiah Thomas's accusation of stereotyping, has written that he is "still waiting for an apology." ESPN's Dick Vitale believes the issue has been overblown, and attributes some of the problem to jealousy, to "nitpicking," and to people who are "always taking shots." "I think people try to make something bigger than it really is," he says. "I know it doesn't happen to me. I know definitely. Let's just leave that out. Let's just play ball."

Through the years there have been several studies on the racial content of sports reporting. Most recently, *Boston Globe* columnist Derrick Z. Jackson analyzed the linguistic content of seven televised NFL playoff games and five NCAA basketball games during the 1988–89 season. He classified broadcasters' comments according to categories he called "brawn" (running, leaping, size, and quickness), "brains" (intelligence, leadership, and motivation), "weakling" (lack of speed and size), and "dunce" (being confused or out of emotional control). Statistics were compiled by researchers who had not watched or listened to the games.

Jackson found that in football, while 60 percent of the starting players were black, black athletes received 87 percent of the "brawn" comments and 90 percent of all "dunce" comments. Whites received 67 percent of "brain" comments and 86 percent of all "weakling" comments (such as "He doesn't have the physical talent, but . . ."). The statistics compiled from the college-basketball games were remarkably similar.

"Network sports is where racism is the thickest," says Pluria Marshall. "If you looked at the top fifty executives around network sports they're probably all white." Marshall isn't too far off. According to Susan Kerr, a network spokesperson, CBS Sports has a black vice president in charge of accounting, but no black producers or directors. And as of April 1988, NBC Sports had a single black vice president, one producer, and no directors, a spokesperson for that network reported.

For the most part, rather than hire black broadcasters, the networks feel more comfortable with white ex-coaches, fiftyish men who imitate street slang as a means of establishing a semblance of personal rapport with tall blacks in their teens and twenties. As evidence of their unusual sensitivity to blacks, these coaches are quick to point to their prolonged, frequent contact with blacks. ("I was the first guy ever to recruit a black guy into the ACC," says CBS's Billy Packer; "When I coached the [Detroit] Pistons, we supposedly had the first all-black team in the NBA," says ESPN's basketball analyst Dick Vitale.) But coaches establish a relationship with players—black or white—mainly by controlling them, initially by sizing them up like stock and eventually by offering or withholding the lifeblood of scholarships, contracts, and playing time. At best, all the forced street jive is merely embarrassing to watch; at worst, a public paternalism seeps in, as with Vitale's treatment of college player Derrick Coleman.

"Derrick Coleman, now he's really a good kid," Vitale assured the nation one evening in 1988. "But he should open up a little more and let you get to know him." It was an offhand comment, made during a pause in the action, one of many such instant portraits Vitale rendered that evening. He was speaking of a tall black teenager from urban Detroit who plays basketball for Syracuse University. Interviewed several weeks later, Vitale was asked how well he really knew Derrick Coleman and why any viewer should have presumed, before alerted, that Coleman was anything but a good kid.

"Well," says Vitale, "I've done seven Syracuse games. I've watched 'em at practice. I've spoken at Syracuse banquets. Once I brought him [Coleman] over and tried to show some people who thought he was not a good kid, I said, 'Look at this kid, now this is not a bad kid.' I said, 'This kid here just happens to be a little quiet. I sat for hours in the front of a plane to Alaska with

Coleman and those guys goin' to Alaska, bullthrowin'. Think you don't get to know a guy flyin' to Alaska?"

Vitale's CBS counterpart Billy Packer, as both a coach's son and an ex-coach himself, is more of a technocrat, an X and O guy, than Vitale, or NBC's Al McGuire, an ex-coach for Marquette. Packer prides himself as an accurate commentator. He wants you to be able to bank on his descriptions and insights. In 1988, Packer was singled out by *Washington Post* columnist Michael Wilbon, who is black, for what Wilbon considered Packer's exclusive association of the word "athlete" with blacks. "Billy Packer, week in, week out, is as bad as anyone on television in perpetuating stereotypes," Wilbon wrote. "Turn away from the TV set and listen to Packer. 'What an athletic move!' means a black player made the shot. 'What a smart, gutty decision that was!' means a white player hit it."

Billy Packer thinks it's a bum rap. "Anytime I mention that a guy has great athletic ability," he says, "I'm not demeaning the other characteristics he may also have, like work ethic or intelligence."

Random House's Dictionary of the English Language, second edition, defines an "athlete" as "a person trained or gifted in exercises or contests involving physical agility, stamina, or strength; a participant in a sport, excercise, or game requiring physical skill." That's not what Packer means. "Webster didn't define 'athlete' in terms of basketball," Packer says after hearing the above definition. "If you got the top ten brains of basketball and said, 'Explain to me what are the athletic qualities of a basketball player,' I guarantee you that definition would fall into quickness, leaping ability, speed, and power.' There aren't many [whites], to be honest, in terms of pure athletic ability. . . . I wouldn't argue that eye-hand coordination is not an athletic skill, but that's not the total thing. You could have that and not be able to play. You could have that and be in a wheelchair. So you're not a player. It takes more than that to be an athlete."

Vitale is another broadcaster who rarely associates the word "athlete" with white players in his broadcasts. And he likewise says he doesn't see a lot of white athletes in his profession. "If a kid takes off flying through the sky and he hangs up in the air à la Michael Jordan, heck, he's a bona-fide athlete. Whaddaya gonna say about it? . . . Then you got that big slow kid comin' down who can't jump over the telephone book, and he just so happens, when you look, to be white. You get the point? It just so happens that the white kid isn't the great jumper, isn't the super-quick kid, doesn't have the ultralateral quickness. There-fore, you say to yourself, 'Why is he in a uniform?' Well, he's there because basically he has a pretty good touch, because he makes some intelligent plays on the floor. That's what you hear out of analysts. I don't think it's a racist comment. I just think it's an honest comment."

The problem is that blacks don't, after a game, remember their play as a series of explosions or random flights. Asked about their experience, they talk about what they were trying to do, and the effort that went behind it, just like the "intelligent" whites. To describe Michael Jordan as "a kid who takes off flying through the sky," as Dick Vitale does, is to lose sight of the person who decided to spring. The jump, and the direction and timing of the jump, were strategic decisions, made in microseconds, based on years of practice, of trial and error, of theory developed on play-grounds and in gyms.

Billy Packer, previewing the Syracuse-Indiana game for the 1987 NCAA basketball championship, contrasted two star guards—Indiana's Steve Alford, who is white, and Syracuse's Sherman Douglas, who is black, as follows: "Steve Alford is a guy who's extremely patient. He's a great shooter. A senior. A guy who constantly moves without the ball. On the other side ya got the impatient athlete, the superathlete in Sherman Douglas. He has the ball in his hands all the time. He's a street fighter."

A few months later, Douglas heard Packer's description for the first time and was asked if the words struck him as an accurate description of himself. "Well no," Douglas said thoughtfully. "In my case I just had a desire to win. I would just say I'm 'gutty' and 'I like to win' . . . I don't really think I'm a superathlete. I know I'm quick. I know there are certain things I really can't do on the court." Asked if he had ever been in a street fight, Douglas laughed softly. "Well, no, not a 'street fight,' " he said. "Sometimes they classify black athletes like that, you know, 'street fighter.' I just play hard every game. I've never seen Billy Packer around where I live. They don't know where I'm from."

The great shot-blocker Bill Russell once described his personal experience of a great leap. "One of [Stanford's] players stole the ball at half-court for a breakaway lay-up," Russell wrote. "He was so far ahead of us that nobody bothered to chase him but me. The guy's lead was so big he wasn't hurrying. When I reached half-court I took one long stride off to the left to change my angle, then went straight for the bucket. I was flying . . . the sweetness of the play was the giant step I took to the left as I was building up speed. Without that step the play would have failed, because I'd have fouled the guy by landing on him after the shot. The step to the left gave me just enough angle coming across to miss him and land to the right of him without a foul. K.C. [Jones, his teammate] was the only guy in the Cow Palace who noticed that step and knew what it meant."

Many people watching the game probably were watching the shooter and saw Russell's leap as an event of spontaneous combustion, as a body exploding out of nowhere like a hot kernel of popcorn. Most great leapers, black or white, are not as articulate as Russell in describing the jumps they make, but that doesn't mean they happen without an accompanying idea.

Likewise, Oscar Robertson, a black man who perhaps mastered basketball more completely than anyone, was described in one history of college basketball as "so superbly blended and proportioned (and driven by such a fission-fast nervous system) that he achieved the graceful, swift appearance of a large, lithe cat." While he is quite willing to acknowledge his considerable ability, Robertson once described the construction of his game in a way that had more to do with the mind of an engineer than the body of a cat. "I worked a lot alone," he said. "I thought about situations in a game. I dribbled around chairs and and worked on my crossover and change-of-pace dribbles. I ran into stationary objects and faked one way and went another way. It was like a baseball player standing in front of a mirror with a bat and watching his swing. But I think my most important improvement came in competition, in the battle. In actual competition you have to react to what happens to you, and what happens to the defense when you try something. After a while it becomes automatic."

Calvin Hill, a former NFL All-Pro running back, who is black (as were all but two NFL starting running backs in 1987), likens great breakaway runners to jazz improvisers who launch long solo flights from a solid—but unrecognized—foundation of chord theory. "Most good runners know what's happening," he says. "You practice it. Then, in a game, it's not like you stand there and say, 'Well, there's Rayfield Wright, and he's a better blocker than someone else.' You've already thought that out. The program in your brain takes over. Subconsciously you've probably seen and imagined every situation. But it's work. It's all work. That's hard to see sometimes."

Hill thinks stereotypical ways of looking at whites and blacks blind observers to what's really happening. He remembers watching Jerry West, a white player, play a game of one-on-one basket-ball. "He dunked the ball and went behind his back. I was amazed. White people weren't supposed to be able to do that." On the other hand, the qualities of speed and explosiveness, when possessed by a black athlete, can lead to the automatic assumption of great athleticism, while similar qualities in whites are often overlooked. Hill offers his former Cowboy teammates as examples. "[The question in defining a superior athlete is] can an athlete transfer great eye-hand coordination and other qualities to other sports? At Dallas, Charlie Waters was a natural athlete. He could play anything. He was white, and it wasn't really noticed. Roger Staubach was a good athlete, and his athleticism was underrated. But I've known black guys with tremendous speed who were not great athletes, guys like Jim Hines and Mike Pruitt. On the other hand, Bob Hayes [also black] had great speed and was a great athlete."

More than anything innate about black people, it may be that his realization of the American dream has caused the white athlete's decline. Sports has long been seen as a way out of poverty; if you're already out, you no longer need the road. Songwriter Paul Simon asks where Joe DiMaggio—the last white preintegration baseball hero—has gone. He's gone on to a better life; he has options now, and he's less obsessive about any one of them. "In most cases, the athletes of today are black kids," says Gordon Ash, director of minor league operations for the Toronto Blue Jays. "The white guys are out driving their cars and having a pizza. The black guy is practicing his skills." Although much is made of his limited running and jumping ability, Larry Bird probably has more essential things in common with his black peers than with white suburban players like Bill Laimbeer and Danny Ainge and Kiki Vanderweghe and Kelly Tripucka. Bird grew up in a large, poor mobile family headed by a working parent in a community that valued basketball obsessively. As he was growing up, Bird's neighbors in French Lick, Indiana, were not hounding him to major in math. He spent his days and nights practicing basketball.

The portrait of black athletes as spontaneous, unthinking, natural performers—born with an advantage—can be debilitating both to blacks and whites. It can lead young black athletes to imitate the skywalkers at the expense of mastering fundamentals. "Undisciplined—that means nigger," said Georgetown basketball coach John Thompson to *Sports Illustrated* writer Bil Gilbert. "They're all big and fast and can leap like kangaroos and eat watermelon in the locker room, but they can't play as a team and they choke under pressure. It's the idea that a black man doesn't have the intelligence or character to practice self-control. In basketball it's been a self-fulfilling prophecy. A white coach recruits a good black player. . . . He puts him in the free-lance, one-on-one role. Other black kids see this and they think that is how they are expected to play."

For whites, the belief that blacks are born with an advantage can lead to a dampened confidence, a fatalism, a growing feeling that they are hanging on only through guile and superior training techniques. Isiah Thomas, in an interview with Detroit sportswriter Charlie Vincent, described, in essence, a sense of surrender. "In every basketball camp I go to across America," said Thomas, "there is at least one white kid who thinks this black kid can run faster than he can and jump higher than he can simply because he's black and he was born with this God-given gift. . . . Do you know what a sin it is for an eleven-year-old white boy to think that he's got 'white man's disease'? To think he can't run, and to think he's always going to be slow? Do you know what a sin it is to that kid, who really wants to play ball? Better to tell him, 'Hey kid, exercise, lose some weight, run, lift weights.' "

Many whites seem to fear being left out entirely. Of all the forlorn words that Jimmy the Greek said in Duke Zeibert's restaurant, perhaps the most revealing was the wistful observation—that of a kid whose next-door neighbor moved away with the only ball—that if blacks "take over coaching jobs like everybody wants them to, there's not going to be anything left for the white people."

ESPN broadcaster Dick Vitale may have said the same thing even more poignantly with a remark he made about Indiana University's white guard Steve Alford before the Indiana-Syracuse NCAA championship game: "I love Steve Alford for one reason," said Vitale. "He represents America: no size, no speed, no strength."

■

Harold Bell remembers his one shot at a network audition the way boxers remember a single chance for a title fight. "Jim Nantz, who is the sports anchor at [Washington's NBC affiliate television station] WRC just *demanded* that NBC give me an audition," Bell recalls. "So they did. I had written up a commentary, about a five-minute sports piece. Jim had tried to help me, but it was too much. I felt like a fish out of water. They just threw me in cold. I didn't know how to go from camera one to camera two, you know. I didn't know what the monitor was. I'd never had any experience with it, so I'm sure all my split verbs, all my nervousness and stumbling came across. I never got to see that audition. I asked for a copy, so I could use it to improve, and they said, 'Sure, we'll get back to you.' But they never did."

The experience of Bell, a forty-seven-year-old ex–professional wide receiver, is typical of blacks trying to get into sportswriting or broadcasting. For the last fifteen years Bell has bounced around Washington, D.C., as a free-lance sports broadcaster on faint, thousand-watt black-owned AM radio stations. *The Washington*

Post, in declaring Bell's one-hour radio talk show "D.C.'s best" also dubbed it "the best radio show you'll never hear."

Although blacks dominate the playing field, they are all but invisible in the media. In 1984, the American Society of Newspaper Editors reported that 94 percent of all American newsrooms were white, and 97 percent of all news executives. At that time, three fifths of America's papers had no minority reporters at all. Today, almost all of the information you receive about a black athlete through any medium is owned, financed, selected, edited, and delivered by white people.

At this writing, among general-circulation newspapers, there is one black sports columnist in America, Roy Johnson of *The Atlanta Constitution,* who took over the column from another black, Terry Moore. About three fourths of all black sports reporters are funneled into the NBA beat. There were twice as many black quarterbacks in the NFL in 1987–88 (four), than there were black NFL reporters (two). Four black reporters cover major league baseball on a regular basis. *Sports Illustrated,* which has witnessed the black athlete's progress since the early fifties, has had for many years one black reporter—Ralph Wiley—on the staff. Black sports editors and general managers are about as abundant as black NFL head coaches and coordinators, and the reasons why are the same.

Racial stereotypes hound black would-be sportscasters. "Whenever you hear a black who can put a few words together," CBS basketball announcer James Brown once observed, "you're told, 'Here's an *articulate* black.' You never hear about articulate whites." Few potential employers are as candid as one Andy Ockershausen, a white man who is president and general manager of the sports station WFTY in D.C. "Blacks are better athletes than they are communicators," declares Ockershausen. "That's a fact. It's cultural. You can hear it."

Ockershausen is asked how you get to be a good communicator. "Well, you gotta start with the smaller markets and work your way up," he says. "You gotta go to work in smaller cities. They [blacks] haven't paid their dues. They haven't exposed their talent." What about a training program? "Ah, we tried that with a guy a couple of years ago," says Ockershausen. "We busted our ass tryin' to polish him up. He didn't work out. We tried with Kenny Houston too. Then he decided he didn't wanna do it."

For blacks, trying to get into the booth or behind the microphone—or to stay there—has been much like getting in the boardroom or the front office, or behind the center on a football field. Only a few, mostly sports immortals such as Sugar Ray Leonard, Bill Russell, Oscar Robertson, O. J. Simpson, Reggie Jackson, and Maury Wills, have even tasted the wine of a top network sportscasting job. Few have lasted long, or been groomed as personalities. CBS has employed only five black announcers in fifteen years of covering the NBA. "I worked for ABC for eleven or twelve years," Reggie Jackson has said. "In all that time, I hosted one show, a drag race. I thought I did a good job, but no one asked me to host a network show again."

And at the network level, blacks usually get sent down to the losing locker room to interview the losing coach, like ABC's Lynn Swann after the 1988 Super Bowl ("You're very gracious to come back out here, coach. How do you feel?") or CBS's James Brown after the NCAA championships ("What would you do differently, coach?"). Others go to the locker room to flag down injury reports and relay them up to the booth, or, like NBC's Irv Cross, play third fiddle on the halftime show. Still others, from the network's anchor desk, report scores of games whites have broadcast.

Broadcasting jobs often go to ex–head coaches, almost all of whom are white, and to ex-players who starred in controlling positions, where blacks seldom play. While more than three quarters of all black baseball players play first base or outfield, almost all broadcasters—like ABC's Tim McCarver and Jim Palmer and NBC's Tony Kubek and Joe Garagiola—played middle infield, pitcher, or catcher. "In football, it goes coach, quarterback, and you can throw the rest in a general pool," says Ed Jones, who was between 1977 and 1987 the program manager at CBS television affiliate WOR in Washington, D.C. "But who do they have to work with? They will bounce a player to get a coach, like a John Madden, because he has to provide strategy and insight, and the players'll talk to him. But how many black coaches do we have? And how many black quarterbacks?"

Blacks complain that major sports media have not invested in time to groom them, to give them speech training, to teach them the nuances of working on-camera. "I tell the networks that broadcasting is a learned skill," says Jones, who gave sportscasting starts to James Brown and Sugar Ray Leonard. "You can take a black athlete who has a certain ability to communicate, even if the 'you knows' and split verbs are there, and work with them, train them and expose them, and pair them up with a good writer and speaker, and eventually you will cultivate a good communicator.

"White coaches do this with black athletes all the time. They take a black athlete out of a high school in Mississippi, and groom him to perform as a running back or a guard. The networks have to make the same commitments in television positions. They're gonna have to open up their management ranks. They're gonna have to get some black sports producers and associate producers, people who make decisions on the content. Otherwise it's not gonna happen. They gotta want to do it. That's the bottom line. They'll have to groom black sportscasters the way they groomed Dan Rather and Lesley Stahl and Diane Sawyer. The early Bryant Gumbel wasn't nearly as good as he is now. After a while, even that guy on *Broadcast News* will learn.

"Actually, I think the colleges and universities may be hurting kids more than the networks," Jones adds. "I'm just waiting for one of these kids to file a suit against a major university based on their broadcasting degree. They're ripping the kids off. Many football and basketball players are majoring in mass communications. That's because it's an easy degree. Universities can bury athletes where the demands are not as high. They give the students a lot of theory and no skills. So a lot of young people are trying to get into media and there's no jobs. It's exactly like sports."

In 1968 the Kerner report, a study of racial relations in the United States, described the news media as "shockingly backward in seeking out, hiring, training, and promoting Negroes," and scored them for "ignoring the underlying racial tensions in American society." Twenty years later, the main thing that has changed is that the word "Negro" doesn't get used much anymore.

For the most part, the major sports media have discouraged discussion about minority hiring, or about their role in the continuing estrangement between blacks and whites. Jimmy "the Greek" Snyder's words "do not reflect in any way the thinking or attitudes of the rest of us at CBS Sports," said Brent Musburger, after Snyder's Last Words. "People forget, Bryant Gumbel was our baseball pregame host and Ahmad Rashad is on *NFL Live!*" said Michael Weissman, executive director of NBC Sports, responding to an inquiry about minority hiring.

Billy Packer is asked if CBS ever discusses the issue of racial stereotypes with its broadcasters. "Nope," he says. "You'd probably be shocked—the networks never discuss anything in the form of critique. I can't speak for the other networks but CBS has no policy coming off the Jimmy 'the Greek' statements. They had no policy coming off the Tom Brookshier statements. . . . [In 1983, during a CBS college-basketball broadcast, Brookshier, an ex-professional football player, remarked that the University of Louisville team had "a collective IQ of about forty, but they can play basketball."] To me, it's like [they're saying] 'Hey, this'll go away. You know? Don't fool with it.' I think it's bullshit when you have a topic that is obviously an issue that can be addressed, and where you could come out with a positive answer. That's not the way you grow in appreciation of the other guy's position. The way you grow is to discuss your opinion as opposed to his, and then come out with some common understanding."

If the growing number of black athletes continue to be described almost exclusively by white reporters, it is likely that viewers and readers will continue to be denied a realistic picture of their minds, tactics, desires, motives, and plans for success. "The point isn't just to hire blacks to talk to blacks," says Larry Whiteside, a black reporter for *The Boston Globe.* "But if Jim Rice feels more comfortable talking to a black reporter, he should have that opportunity. Many of the writers who come from a white environment are not sensitive to what black guys are talking about."

O W N E R S H I P :

F O R A

P I E C E O F

T H E P I E

"Someone asked me today whom I would rather be, President U. S. Grant of the United States or President Champion of the Cincinnati Red Stockings baseball club. I immediately answered him that I would by far rather be the President of the Red Stockings."
—AARON B. CHAMPION, PRESIDENT OF THE FIRST
PROFESSIONAL BASEBALL CLUB, FOUNDED IN 1869

Several months before the 1984 Olympic Games were to begin, Ken Shropshire, a black Los Angeles–based attorney working with the Los Angeles Olympic Organizing Committee, was assigned to set up the two-week-long boxing event at the Los Angeles Memorial Sports Arena. His job was to hire all the vendors, ticket and program printers, transportation companies, cleaning crews, waste-disposal outfits, security guards, and parking-lot concessionaires.

Shropshire had assumed that here would be a good opportunity to hire minority firms, to offer them a piece of the Olympic pie. After all, he reasoned, all U.S. boxers in all eleven weight classes were black, and the Sports Arena was publicly owned, which meant affirmative-action guidelines and minority representation. He was wrong: "The stage was already set," recalls Shropshire, now an associate professor at the Wharton School of Business. "The Sports Arena people just handed me a list and said, 'These are the people we use.' I encountered no black people in charge of anything. Not security, not concessions. Nothing. The Sports Arena people had no blacks on their staff, except for one ex–L.A. Ram who went around and gave people tours. Not one black person came in to say, 'This is my company and I can do this for you.' There were some black security guards, and blacks selling peanuts, but in terms of management people, people getting large sums of money, I just didn't run across any."

By far the most important statistic in the history of black participation in American sports—mightier than Hank Aaron's 755 home runs, or Wilt's 100 points or Walter Payton's yardage totals or Florence Griffith-Joyner's dashes, more durable even than Bob Beamon's impossible leap—is that since 1869, when Aaron Champion's Cincinnati Red Stockings first took the field, no black person has ever owned even a share of a major league sports team in America. In all that time, except for those who ran the Negro baseball leagues, no black has ever had a serious financial stake in an integrated professional sports team's destiny.

Sports executives have been quick to point out that the sports segment of the entertainment industry is no different or no worse, in terms of minority control, than any other major American industry. But there is one major difference: Increasingly, in professional and major college sports, the black athlete is the product being sold.

Even counting the enormous salaries that a few black athletes earn, there are many other nonathletes earning more from a given event, and almost all of these people are white. Stadiums and arenas are owned and controlled by whites. Very few major contracts for concessions have ever been granted to black-owned companies. All of the boards of all of the companies buying television time, and of the networks themselves, are either exclusively white or controlled by whites.

One of the most lucrative of the cottage industries attending big-time sports is player representation. Agents compete bitterly for big-name athletes and for the standard 10 percent cut of a major contract. It hasn't been easy for them to find endorsements for black athletes, or to get top dollar. In a 1988 survey, Market Evaluations, Inc., a firm that rates the attractiveness of celebrities, found that the seven most appealing athletes in the world were black. And yet only one (Michael Jordan) of the twelve highest-paid athletes in terms of commercial endorsements was black. Somehow, Jack Nicklaus, Ivan Lendl, and even retired race-car driver Jackie Stewart were easier sells than Magic Johnson or Eric Dickerson. According to *The Wall Street Journal,* in the year after Doug Williams became the Super Bowl MVP, he earned $175,000, compared to the $750,000 that Super Bowl quarterback Phil Simms won in 1987 and $1 million plus that Jim McMahon pulled in the year before.

Black agents have struggled to become established. "The amount of infighting and nastiness is tremendous among the *majority* people," says Fred Slaughter, America's senior black agent. "You know what it's like when there's a minority trying to get into the club."

Slaughter was the burly six-foot-five center on John Wooden's first UCLA championship team. He decided, after picking up a law degree in 1970 at Columbia to go with his MBA, that what he really wanted to do was represent basketball players. He doesn't remember the early days with special fondness. "When I started out in the business, it was like a country club," Slaughter recalls. "We could work in the kitchen but not get in the club. I was isolated. There were no role models. I had absolutely no one to turn to."

It took him until 1974 to land his first big-name client, fellow UCLA alum Jamaal Wilkes, and ever since Slaughter has been patiently kindling a West Coast–based client roster that today includes NBA stars Clyde Drexler, Norm Nixon, Dennis Johnson,

Lafayette Lever, and Michael Cooper. Slaughter believes the color of his skin has never stopped working against him. "The management and representation areas get characterized as a 'white man's domain,' " says Slaughter. "They just tell the kid, 'Only a white man can make that deal for you.' They have actually said that. And some kids, kids who are sitting in a well-furnished office with computers clicking and listening to a guy with gold teeth say that, they'll think, 'Wait a minute: If he's sayin' that, he must be right.' There are a lot of problems. It's been rough."

At first, the sheer precipice of capital formation was enough to keep all but a few enterprising black Americans out of the money end of sports. Before the civil rights movement of the 1950s and 1960s, there were two principal ways for blacks to get big sums of money: They could either entertain white people or seize control of the neighborhood numbers or "policy" game. The most successful entrepreneurs of the Negro baseball leagues, most notably Gus Greenlee, owner of the Pittsburgh Crawfords, and Abraham Manley, who owned the Newark Eagles among other teams, were numbers men. While millions of whites wagered on Wednesday-night bingo games and Nevada offered legal gambling for those who could afford to be there, to play the numbers was a crime. To seize control of a policy operation took brains, cunning, guts, timing, boldness, and luck.

Even though organized Negro baseball grew into a $2 million-a-year business during World War II—perhaps America's biggest black-dominated industry at the time—few clubs owned parks or could control their scheduling. Most lost money. After white major league owners raided the teams for their black stars in the late forties and early fifties, Negro baseball—still America's only extensive experience with black team ownership—quickly died. Abraham Manley estimated that he recovered only about 5 percent of his original investment in the Newark Eagles.

Black sports entrepreneurs have achieved real, enduring economic clout only in boxing. The first blacks to make big money, were also numbers men. John Roxborough and Julian Black, friends and colleagues in a Detroit numbers operation, became Joe Louis's managers in 1935. Gus Greenlee owned a stable of boxers in the thirties that included light-heavyweight champion John Henry Lewis. Decades later, Herbert Muhammad, son of Black Muslim leader Elijah Muhammad, managed Muhammad Ali during his years of greatest glory and still manages former welterweight champ Donald Curry. Butch Lewis, who signed Michael and Leon Spinks almost immediately after they won gold medals in the 1976 Olympic Games, is one of boxing's top—and richest—promoters. Emmanuel Steward is the millionaire owner of Kronk Boxing in Detroit.

The man atop boxing's hill today is Don King, a black, fifty-six-year-old former Cleveland numbers kingpin who was convicted of killing one of his runners in a 1967 scuffle. Released from prison in 1971, King got started in the fight business by purchasing a share of heavyweight Ernie Shavers for $8,000. In 1974, King somehow talked Zaire's president Mobutu Sese Seko into putting up $10 million to finance the Muhammad Ali–George Foreman fight in Zaire. After Ali's victory, King became Ali's regular promoter and by 1984, *The New York Times* had estimated Don King's net worth at $45 million. He says he has promoted more title fights than all his predecessors combined.

King regards boxing, for all its troubles, as *the* equal-opportunity sport. "How many professions do you know of," King asked writer Thomas Hauser, "where a black businessman—I said businessman, not athlete or rock-star singer—can come in, and without a college education make one hundred or two hundred thousand dollars?"

Today, even with professional franchises going for $60 million and $70 million apiece, capital is no longer the main obstacle for blacks who wish to aquire teams. According to *Black Enterprise* magazine, the net worth of today's top one hundred black-controlled corporations is well over $4 billion. Black firms have made serious inroads in the construction, health-care, computer, and manufacturing industries. The seventies and eighties have spawned hundreds of black millionaires.

But even though many blacks—including wealthy ex-athletes like Reggie Jackson, Walter Payton, and Julius Erving—have expressed interest in acquiring franchises, there still are no black ownerships in major sports. It hasn't been for lack of trying. After his group's $70 million bid for the Baltimore Orioles was rejected in favor of a white group, Raymond V. Hagsbert, black chief executive officer of the Parks Sausage Company, expressed his bitterness to the *Baltimore Evening Sun.* "Our bid was not rejected," he said. "It just was not considered. We're very disappointed. . . . Not to have the kind of pluralism in ownership that we have on the playing field is very disappointing and shouldn't continue." In 1980, a group that included black former major league star Donn Clendenon secured a ninety-day option to purchase the Oakland Athletics for slightly more than $10 million. Clendenon's partners included two white-controlled firms, who would have put up about 60 percent of the money. Just to make sure, Clendenon had his attorney inquire whether 40-percent minority ownership of a major league team would be acceptable to the committee of team owners who had to ratify the sale. It wasn't. "[An] executive for major league baseball thought fifteen percent [ownership of the A's] would be acceptable, but when he presented it to some of the owners, it was reduced to ten percent or even lower," recalls Clendenon, who now practices law in Sioux Falls, South Dakota. "We let the option expire and Levi Strauss bought the Athletics. We had about forty percent. Why exercise the option when it was gonna fall through?"

Baseball's Reggie Jackson has likewise expressed a desire to marry his fortune to bigger fortunes in an effort to secure a major league team, again preferably in Oakland. "The money is the easiest thing to work out," Jackson told *Sports Illustrated* in 1987. "People in the front office must be willing to give me a certain amount of power." According to Clendenon, who has continued trying to buy a franchise since his Oakland option expired, Jackson needn't hold his breath. Asked if it's any better now, Clendenon laughs. "How many blacks own pieces of major league baseball?" he asks in return. "I rest my case."

The NBA—77 percent of whose players were black in 1988—has been the league where blacks have penetrated deepest into management. The league has several black head coaches and two black general managers. And as part of his long-term contract with the Sacramento Kings basketball team, Bill Russell—who was also the first black NBA head coach and one of the first black network sports announcers—now has the option to become part owner of the club after seven years.

Still, even in the NBA, ownership has been a closed door. Don King tried to buy the Cleveland Cavaliers when owner Ted Steptien announced its sale. King believes the town recoiled in horror at the prospect of King's control. "They went out and got the [white] Gund brothers," King told the *Plain Dealer*. "The same thing happened to Ed DeBartolo [when he tried to buy the Cleveland Indians]. They didn't want Italians and they didn't want blacks." In 1988 a group headed by black Boston entrepreneur Bertram Lee abandoned an effort to aquire the NBA's San Antonio Spurs, after being, as an observer told *The Boston Globe*, "nickel and dimed to death," by Spurs owner Angelo Drossos.

The NFL is the bleakest of a dismal lot, with no head coaches or significant black executives in the league's history. (The Washington Redskins, the last NFL team to integrate, did so in 1962 only in the face of a court order that threatened to suspend federal funds for construction of a new stadium. "We'll start signing Negroes," Redskins owner George Marshall once cracked, "when the Harlem Globetrotters start signing whites.")

For the past eight years, a group of black businessmen, including former running back Gale Sayers, has been carefully positioning itself for a bid on an NFL expansion team, should one ever become available. They anticipate a price tag as high as $60 million, but it's worth it to them. "It's all about owning something in America," says Dr. Robert E. Lee, a Tallahassee-based broadcaster who heads the group. "If you can't participate in ownership, you can't participate in our free-enterprise system. It's not about a football team, it's about owning something. That's the name of the game. Coaching's just a job. The only way to penetrate the system is to get a piece of the action."

Black America has had a single, brief experience with ownership of a farm team in major league baseball, an affair that ended recently in Savannah, Georgia. One group of entrepreneurs tried it the old-fashioned American way. They bought in at the bottom and set out to work their way up to the majors. They were determined and patient, and invested enough money to make it work. They wanted to gain experience, to fashion a network of contacts that would give them an insider's chance to own a major league franchise someday.

In 1986 Thomas Lewis, chairman of Inter-Urban Broadcasting, Inc., a Chicago-based entertainment conglomerate, bought the Savannah Cardinals, the St. Louis Cardinals' Class A club in the South Atlantic ("Sally") League. And while Inter-Urban's staff expected that the intrusion of a group of black managers into an ancient Georgia baseball franchise would be a little jarring, race played an even bigger role than anyone could have thought.

■

Tom Lewis had spent too much time working to develop a boy-
hood interest in sports. He started by delivering papers on Chicago's West Side as a kid, and by disguising his age he managed
to hustle his own truck route long before he was sixteen. Even as
a teenager, moonlighting was his way of life. He worked his way
through college, got a teaching certificate, and bought a fuel
truck, from which he delivered heating oil after school.

He left the classroom and took a job at a large black-owned bank
in Chicago, and soon had his own South Side bank and a substan-
tial line of credit. After he and a partner bought their first radio
station, in Gary, Indiana, they kept on moonlighting, spending
their evenings in Gary learning the radio business. By the age of
fifty-two, when he bought the Savannah Cardinals, Tom Lewis
was a tough and straightforward entrepreneur who had leveraged
that Gary station into, among other assets, seven radio stations
and two car-rental franchises.

The notion of buying a baseball team had first entered Lewis's
mind during a chance meeting in Louisville with A. Ray Smith,
a portly old silver-haired promoter often likened in print to P. T.
Barnum. In 1982 Smith had bought the Louisville Redbirds, a St.
Louis Cardinals Triple A farm team, and had quickly transformed
it into a bonanza. By 1984 the Redbirds became the first minor
league team ever to draw a million fans. They had outdrawn three
major league teams, and A. Ray Smith had become a civic hero
in Louisville.

All he had done, Smith explained to Tom Lewis, was sink some
money into restoring the stadium—which he likened to Dunkirk
after the war—and promote the hell out of baseball. You had to
get the corporations involved, like the nights in Louisville when
a supermarket chain paid for all the seats and gave away free
groceries. He kept the ticket prices low and made money by

running his own concessions rather than contracting them out. He had an attraction, like fireworks or the San Diego chicken, every night. He made it fun. And the beauty of it was that St. Louis put up the real money. He was just the franchise owner. *They* paid the salaries and handled all the player headaches. There is no reason, A. Ray Smith liked to say, why any baseball team should ever lose money at any level.

About a month later Tom Lewis noticed an ad in *The Wall Street Journal.* Savannah Cardinals, Class A, South Atlantic League, $285,000. He called, but was told that a sale was imminent. When they called him back to tell him the deal had fallen through, he jumped on a plane, and he bought the Savannah Cardinals the next day.

To Tom Lewis, it didn't matter so much that the previous owner, a Kentucky businessman named Will May, had lost a small fortune on the team, and that nobody, not even a Double A farm team of the local heroes, the Atlanta Braves, had ever managed to make money in Savannah. What mattered was that Savannah, Georgia, had all the ingredients: 220,000 people and no other minor league team closer than Charleston, South Carolina. There was a big stadium, available from the city at ten grand a year. And this was a Cardinals franchise, too, just like A. Ray Smith's Louisville Redbirds. St. Louis would pay all the coaches and players. How much could they lose?

And there was more to it than that: Here was a chance to break some new ground. Even more than radio, professional sports was a desert for black management, a wasteland where a few black ex-players had jobs as low-level coaches or "special assistants." Tom Lewis had on his staff a manager who could make it happen, a smart, energetic, and profoundly underemployed young talent in New Orleans who had told him she wanted to get serious about business.

Tracy Lewis, then twenty-five, will never forget her father's call.

"He seemed very excited," she recalls. "He was talking fast, saying, 'We bought a baseball team, right out of *The Wall Street Journal.*' And then he said, 'And you're the president.'" He told her when to meet him in Savannah to "get set up." "No problem," she heard herself say.

■

Despite having grown up six blocks from Chicago's Comiskey Park, Tracy Lewis had been to only two baseball games in her life. Later, when writers kept asking her about them, she realized she couldn't actually remember either one. The elder child of professionals—her mother is dean of students for the School of Social Work at the University of Illinois at Chicago—hers was a girlhood of Montessori schools and opera and ballet lessons and piano recitals. When her father telephoned, Tracy had been cooling out in New Orleans, managing the personnel department of his New Orleans radio station. She had just dropped out of Tulane Law School, which had been boring, and found herself content for a while to listen to people complain all day until her life's calling presented itself. That it would be "baseball club president" had not occurred to her, but she was willing to try.

When she arrived in Savannah and found her office in a trailer underneath the third-base grandstand at Savannah's William L. Grayson Stadium, she sat down and began returning phone calls. At the top were several from a man named Max Patkin. He answered right away. In a hurried voice he said he still had a few open dates in July; when did she want him? Tracy was silent. "Do you know who I am?" Patkin finally asked. Tracy said, "No." Patkin said, "Oh, my God," twice. Then he told her he was the Clown Prince of Baseball.

A few days later, the SavCards' holdover general manager—Tracy's only help—scribbled a forwarding address and announced from the trailer doorway that he was leaving—at once—to become the general manager of a team closer to his hometown. The thing that amazed Tracy most was that he had been able to find another front-office job so quickly. He couldn't have been looking long, she thought. Still, the bottom line was she was on her own. He had known everything about baseball. She knew next to nothing.

It was February and she was alone, deep under baseball's hood. Twenty-four players would be arriving in seven weeks. She was awash in details, each a revelation. For one thing, it turned out *she* would have to provide their balls and bats. If this were a symphony, she asked herself, would the musicians show up without their instruments?

Vendors, sensing fresh blood, were everywhere. Paper-cup salesmen. Napkins. Cleaning fluid. Paper towels. She despised the insurance agents. They wanted $11,000 for a blanket liability policy. What if a fan slips in a puddle of beer? they asked her. What if a foul ball puts out an infant's eye? Suppose somebody collapses in the bleachers? The bus company wanted $17,000 to transport players around the South for four months. The city wanted $11 an hour to stake three cops at the games.

She hustled Savannah nonstop, courting the mayor, the television stations, and the corporations, improvising promotional events, and hawking outfield billboard space at $1,000 a board. She saturated the black community with fliers. Sandy James, a saleswoman on loan from Tom Lewis's radio network, went to a different church every Sunday, leaving a contribution in the plate and a stack of SavCard brochures in the lobby.

Just before opening day, Tracy flew with one of her father's accountants to St. Louis to go over the "player development contract" with Paul Fox and Lee Thomas, executives of the St. Louis Cardinals. During the flight, she found herself anxious about projecting self-confidence. It was hard to shake the novelty of her experience: She had rarely given baseball a thought. These guys, she assumed, had spent a lifetime in the game; they'd probably met in a dugout or an infield somewhere.

Fox and Thomas were polite as Tracy grilled them about the contract. The bottom line, they said, was that the Lewises were responsible for providing a stadium, concessions, and an atmosphere in which to develop baseball players. For that they got to keep the gate. In return, the St. Louis Cardinals would provide baseball players, a manager, and coaches. The Lewises would have no say about who those people were or how long any of them would stay in Savannah. The Savannah Cardinals, Fox and Thomas explained, were what you called a "low A" team. It turned out that St. Louis had three Class A teams while most major league clubs had just two. In effect, Savannah's roster contained the least promising of the Cards' Class A prospects. You might not win much down there, they said. They also told her the contract gave her one hundred boxes of free baseballs, thirty-six balls to a box. The rest of the balls, they said, were up to the Lewises.

On April 6, 1986, thirty-nine years after the first black major league player had trotted out to second base for the Brooklyn Dodgers, the first black-owned major league farm club took the field in Savannah, Georgia. Four thousand people showed up for what the mayor called "Pack the Park Night" in Grayson Stadium. The crowd was over a tenth of the previous year's total attendance, a promising testament to what Tracy had managed to accomplish in three short months.

After she flung out the opening pitch, sending the catcher lunging to his left, Tracy signaled for the special event that would herald a big new era of fun for SavCard baseball.

For this occasion Tracy had hired an ex-marine to climb into the team's bright-red fuzzy Cardinal costume and parachute into Grayson Stadium. He had assured her that he had done this kind of thing before, and that, for her, he'd do it for gas money. The regular mascot had objected furiously, claiming that the beak chipped easily, but Tracy insisted.

On cue, as necks craned and Tom Lewis's camera clicked away proudly, a small plane appeared over the stadium and the black dot plunged out. The parachute opened, and seconds later, the jumper landed lightly near home plate—without the bird's head. Tracy rushed into the trailer and put her head down on her arms, awaiting the season's first liability claim. The phone rang. It was Burger King. They had found a Cardinal head outside their drive-up window.

■

Nineteen eighty-six was a marvelous year. They passed the previous year's attendance total by late July and revenues exceeded all expectations. Like A. Ray Smith, Tracy and the staff dreamed up a promotion for almost every home game. She gave away a trip to Belgium, an air conditioner, two ceiling fans, bats, batting gloves, helmets, dinners at Shoneys, lunch dates with players. There was Nostalgia Night, Beacher Bleacher Day, and of course Gnat Night, when anyone named Nat got in free, marking the springtime weeks when hordes of gnats rise from the marshes and descend on outdoor Savannah. Almost every major company in town had a night.

She shared a world of camaraderie with the white mom-and-pop owners of the other Sally League teams, with people like Len and Ann Monheimer of the Macon Pirates and Junior Ramsey of the Spartanburg Phillies. When such folks ran out of hot-dog buns, they raced over to Krogers to get more. They all watched the games with one eye on the field and another on the ushers, wishing to God they would *sell* and not just drift through the aisles, and wondering if they could make change, or if they could count at all. Every home run that flew out of the park was a mixed blessing, a mark on the scoreboard and another $4 down the drain. Whenever one of the SavCards would break a bat, Tracy would cup her hands and yell, "That's twelve dollars!"

If the day in the trailer hadn't been too grinding, Tracy usually made an entrance around the third inning of home games. When she did, heads swiveled. Kids raced down to hang on her, and nearly everyone came by sooner or later to chat.

The stands were studded with characters, mostly fans who had bonded originally to the Savannah Pirates, White Sox, Senators, Astros, Indians, or Braves—former incarnations who had played ball in Grayson Stadium since 1928. A man named Phillips, an ex-umpire, ignored the players and heckled the umpires. "Mean Gene" came only to ride the home team. One night a diehard fan known only as "Frank" stood outside the stadium entrance and began screaming as loud as he could. No one could stop or comfort him. When the gatekeeper went for the police, Frank calmly took over his post and waved scores of people in for free.

One big-boned young woman named Tia came in with a different hairstyle nearly every game. She sat directly behind the screen speaking softly to the players, who were clearly attentive. She once changed outfits three times in a single game, probably a Sally League record. It reached the point in midseason that "Tia's Syndrome" became the presumed cause of any prolonged slump at the plate or wild streak by a pitcher.

The Lewises brought a sense of black pride to Sally League baseball. No longer did fans hear "Thank God I'm a Country Boy" on the stadium loudspeaker between innings. Now it was the Temps, the Miracles, and the Supremes. Most of the vendors, ushers, and concessionaires were black. And except for Mike

Blaser, a twenty-five-year-old sports-management major from a Kentucky college whom Tracy hired as a general manager (and who all season long struggled to answer the question from fans "How come you're not black?"), all of the members of Tracy's front-office team were black.

Tracy found herself drawn to the players. She took them to dinner, drank with them, listened as a friend to their problems, and gave them counsel. It didn't matter that only one of them was black. They were like her, dreamers, risk takers, guys who, by the time they reached her age, twenty-five, were considered by St. Louis to be lost causes. They made $800 a month, took cheap apartments with five or six roommates, and looked for jobs in the off-season with UPS or a gas station, someone who would let them go back in the spring. Each summer they played 140 games with three days off, except when it rained.

One in a hundred had his dream come true. And yet, every one of them was convinced that he was the one who would make it to Busch Stadium. It was because St. Louis had no left-handed middle-inning relief, they told her, or because Ozzie Smith had to fade someday, or because St. Louis needed right-handed power. They told her about the hitches in their swings, the trouble they had going to their right, confided to her that they were thinking about standing farther back in the box. The pitchers seemed the most easily upset, sometimes thrown into funks for days between starts.

When St. Louis released the ballplayers, sometimes they came to her, trying to hold back tears, to say good-bye or fish for a front-office job. She told them, and she believed it sincerely, that they should be proud to be among the few people who would never have to ask themselves what would have happened had they pursued their dreams.

By season's end, Tracy and her collegues had put forty-seven thousand bodies in Grayson Stadium, an average of about seven hundred fans per game. It didn't matter to Tracy, or her father, that forty-seven thousand people would not fill Busch Stadium in St. Louis; what mattered was that attendance and revenues had risen steadily and that they had all learned a great deal. Most of the outfield billboards had been sold and it looked like they would all be sold again the next year. They had moved the team from tenth to fourth in league attendance. They almost broke even in their first year, and were well ahead of schedule. Like A. Ray, they had made it fun.

Most important, the Lewises had made history. They were pioneers, even if hardly anyone in organized baseball seemed to know or care. It was a start and they had done it. *Black Enterprise* magazine lauded their breakthrough in a giddy piece in which St. Louis executives praised Tracy's management style and Tom Lewis allowed that he might be in the market for a major league franchise. Buoyed by the trial balloon, Inter-Urban Broadcasting's board approved plans to sink some serious money into Savannah. They authorized funds to paint the park, take over concessions themselves, and put in Cardinal-red theater seats, and they set out to double revenues in 1987.

■

Four days before the opening game of the 1987 season, Tracy Lewis was en route to Savannah, her head swollen with a miserable cold, probably, she thought, brought on by the stress of trying to get ready for another season. She checked into a motel and struggled to stay awake until 11:30, when *Nightline* was supposed to have a show about Jackie Robinson.

She was almost asleep when somehow she detected a shift in the tone of the conversation. They weren't talking about Jackie Robinson anymore. An old baseball executive was talking. "He was talking about baseball players being fleet of foot, as if they

were racehorses," she recalls. "I sat up and started watching. Even
Ted seemed shocked. You don't usually shock Ted." For her the
punch line came when the baseball guy said that blacks may not
have some of the "necessities" to run a baseball team. That's what
she did. "His facial expression never changed," she recalls. "It
never dawned on him that what he was saying was unacceptable."

The baseball guy, whose name she came to know well, was Al
Campanis, and he had just changed her life with a few words.
Overnight, enterprising journalists discovered that she, Tracy P.
Lewis, was the only black president of an American professional
baseball team. By putting his foot in his mouth on national television, Campanis had quite inadvertently trained a spotlight on the
Savannah Cardinals. The following morning, the sporting world
found out that the most progressive management experience in
the 118-year history of professional baseball was none other than
the Inter-Urban Broadcasting Corporation's nearly invisible attempt to test the baseball market in Savannah, Georgia.

In the weeks and months after Campanis's *Nightline* interview,
the Savannah airport became congested with writers and photog-
raphers on their way in and out. *People* magazine photographed
Tracy floating—to illustrate her buoyancy—and in the dugout
with her arms around a ballplayer. *Newsday* caught her on the
bench, *USA Today* on the phone, and *The Washington Post* at
the bat rack. *The Boston Globe* sent their photo editor to write
the feature story. She came to prefer Greg Gumbel (ESPN) over
his brother Bryant (NBC's *Today*). CBS News and *Sports Illustrated* rang her up, and even the BBC, whose roving reporter had
come to Savannah to do a story on life in an American seaport,
found in Tracy Lewis a better example of Americana.

Of course, Tracy, her father, and their colleagues had long
known they were exotics in baseball's monoculture. The massive
reality of it, of just how different she must look and seem, had not
hit Tracy full force until just a few weeks before, when she had

walked through a revolving door into a Florida hotel lobby to register for baseball's winter meetings and spun into a new world, a world, it turned out, of plaid suits. "They were all white, they were all men, they were all the same age, and they all dressed alike," she recalls.

Interviewers were asking her how she would go about integrating baseball's front offices. She often replied by asking them how they were going about integrating their newsrooms. She told them that baseball should seek résumés of black men and women who had no experience with the game. It's just a business, she said, only the details are different. She used her own staff as an example, pointing to the young black accountants and sales reps and marketers she had assembled. Don't just hire your own, she told them. The real problem in baseball is cronyism.

The new Cardinal-red seats were sprinkled with feature writers who were eager to offer Tracy Lewis—smart, ambitious, attractive, and humane—as living proof that blacks had the "necessities" to control the bottom line. And before their eyes, her team, and its support, began to unravel.

The gate was off from day one. For some reason the mayor, so responsive the year before, was not willing to take part in this year's "Pack the Park" campaign for opening day. On the field, everyone seemed to come down with Tia's Syndrome at once. The team lost twelve of its first fourteen games. The field manager stopped speaking to her. He just wanted to manage, he told Mike Blaser, he didn't want to go out and glad-hand everyone in Savannah, and he wasn't there to be a pioneer.

The fans who had come in such promising numbers at the end of the previous season stayed home emphatically. Nothing could budge them. They stayed home during Nat Night and Beacher Bleacher Day. They avoided Church Program Night. They ignored Tico Brown Autograph Day.

The local newspapers turned negative and sarcastic. Asked why the team was not drawing fans, Donald Heath, a reporter who covered the Cardinals as part of a three-person rotation for the *Savannah Morning News,* cited the Lewises' "complacency." "They rested on their laurels," Heath explained. "They should have had fireworks, a rock band, a bat day, maybe raffled off a car. Tonight I think I'll stay home and rearrange my socks."

Mike Blaser pleaded with St. Louis to send better players to Savannah. One time he thought they were listening when he read that the Cardinals had drafted University of Georgia's ace reliever, Chris Carpenter. "I'm thinking, What a break, what a *break.* I was on the phone to Lee Thomas the day I heard it. I couldn't reach him for two or three days, because he was still drafting other players. I stayed on him. Finally he said, 'We wouldn't send him to you anyway; he'll need more time in rookie ball.' "

With little revenue coming in, the Inter-Urban board took a hard line—they had to find out, they told Tracy, if the baseball team could survive on its own. Bill paying became an exercise in triage. Creditors were starting to complain and the newspapers, by now downright hostile, began to speculate publicly on how long Tom Lewis could or would hold out in Savannah. Staff morale dropped.

Tracy began to develop a sense that, after all the publicity the Campanis episode had generated, Savannah's civic leaders and organized baseball were pulling back from her. The other owners no longer seemed friendly. Last year, she thought, maybe she had been a novelty, and an inconspicuous one at that. Now with all the publicity, with all the pointed advice, maybe she had become a grain of sand in baseball's eye.

Tracy was especially frustrated by St. Louis's behavior. In the wake of Campanis, she thought, they could be crowing about black ownership in Savannah. She felt that by sending attractive players or, at the very least, installing a field manager who wanted to work with her, St. Louis had a chance to help break down some barriers. They could claim to be the most progressive organization in professional sports. But they just didn't seem to care.

Even Savannah's blacks seemed indifferent. "I'll tell ya what the trouble is," said Robert James, a black man who is president of the Carver Bank in Savannah. "Now, I am a baseball fanatic. I watch the [Atlanta] Braves play every night. Now why should I go outside in this heat to watch A ball when I can watch the Braves on cable in air conditioning?"

Others, such as Julius Fine, a white retired judge whose half-century-long involvement in Savannah baseball had caused him to be known locally as "Mr. Baseball," suggested that black ownership had reminded the community of rougher days and set another dynamic in motion. Grayson Stadium had once been the scene of an ugly racial incident that Fine and others feel may have permanently depressed both black and white attendance. "I don't want the Lewises to think I'm against their organization, which I'm not," Fine said during the height of the SavCards' 1987 tailspin. "They all say it's because of television and the beach and other things. I just go along with it."

Grayson Stadium is named for General William L. Grayson, a Spanish-American War veteran and superior court clerk. He is remembered by elderly whites as a top-notch politician, a likable, hand-shaking Democrat, the national commander of the Spanish-American War Veterans. He is remembered by elderly blacks as a rabid segregationist, the man who passed an ordinance that put them in the back of Savannah's streetcars, and who kept Jackie Robinson's Brooklyn Dodgers from playing a 1949 exhibition game in Savannah by declaring he'd tear his name off the stadium wall before a Negro set foot on the field.

Until 1962 all people with dark skin sat together at Grayson Stadium in distant seats down the left-field line, a brick wall separating them from white fans. Blacks relieved themselves in their own restrooms, bought food from black vendors at their own concession stand, drank from their own fountains, bought tickets at their own windows, and entered through their own gate.

Many of Savannah's civil rights activists were also baseball fans, fans who were tired of being stuck out in left field, like their parents and grandparents before them. In the summer of 1962 the Savannah White Sox, led by outfielder Don Buford and a fireballing right-hander named Dave DeBusschere, were locked in a blistering race with Macon for the Sally League flag. Grayson Stadium was an obvious place to organize. After officials of the Savannah White Sox refused to meet with them and the city turned a deaf ear, Savannah NAACP leaders set up a picket line outside the ballpark's main gate and called on all blacks to boycott the games until all facilities were open to all fans.

The first day, hundreds of blacks massed outside the stadium, chanting and picketing the front gate. Then, according to black leaders, Julius Fine, at that time the team's attorney and a major shareholder, obtained the enforcement of a city ordinance that limited the number of picketers to two. "We had to rotate two picketers in and out," recalls W. W. Law. "The haters had a chance to surround you and heckle you. It was very unpleasant. [Picketing] was an act of real courage, because we could not have the support of large numbers."

William Pleasant, a black fan, remembers going out to the ballpark early one evening that summer to paint the outfield billboards with his father. "All of a sudden I heard a whine and looked and there was a bullet hole in the sign, just to the left of me," he recalls.

The picket line soon began to depress attendance. "What really hurt us was that they kept the whites from coming to the games," recalls William Ackerman, a Charleston, South Carolina, attorney who owned the team at the time. "Whites didn't want any trouble." A month before the season ended, Savannah's daily papers published Ackerman's threat to move the team elsewhere unless per-game attendance doubled immediately.

On August 19, 1962, the morning after Julius Fine Night at Grayson Stadium, Ackerman announced that he had accepted an offer of $15,000 to move the team to Lynchburg, Virginia. Fans were stunned. The players packed and left at once for the final homestand in Lynchburg. While the Lynchburg NAACP chapter picketed outside, the 1962 White Sox, had they stayed, would have become Savannah's first professional baseball champions since 1940. Savannah fans went without a baseball team until 1966.

Some in Savannah think that baseball in Savannah still bears the stain of the 1962 boycott and the team's removal. "They [blacks] *had* seats. They had a quarter of the grandstand," says Julius Fine. "When the team came back in sixty-six in an integrated facility, most of the whites quit coming." "They [blacks] didn't gain a thing by it, except to force us to leave town and deprive their black people of the same fun as white people," says Ackerman. "I remember talking to my general manager and he said he was doing everything he could to pacify those people. We were liberals and we wanted the black support."

William Pleasant, now fifty-nine, still paints signs for the Savannah team, now the Cardinals. He is one diehard fan who returned to Grayson Stadium as soon as a team came back to Savannah, and he still sits each night with a small cluster of black fans far down the left-field line, even on nights when Grayson Stadium is nearly empty. He is asked on a slow summer night if he remains in that section because he feels more comfortable away from the white fans, near where he sat in the old days. Looking out at his signs, he finally says, "You know, I guess there could be something to that."

∎

The first and only black owners of a professional sports team affiliated with a major league sold it to the St. Louis Cardinals in November 1987. After the sale, the Cardinals sent public relations people to Savannah to assure interested parties that St. Louis was a "quality organization." Tom Lewis and his partners said that the sale did not represent their retreat from baseball, but rather the recognition that they, like many before them, had not been able to make money running a professional baseball team in Savannah.

Tracy Lewis returned to the radio network, supervising the general managers and the St. Louis station's programming staff. "I would love to get back into baseball," Tracy says. "I'm going to miss it." While she hopes there will be other opportunities, she is not putting the rest of her life on hold waiting for a second chance. "Right now," she says, "out of the whole group, Al Campanis looks like the hero. He can say, 'Well, maybe I shouldn't have said what I said but look at all the good I've done because now everybody's enlightened.' He's got his management class at Berkeley. It's disgusting to me. For major league baseball to let this guy look like a hero is insanity. It shows you where their commitments are."

In April 1988, a year after Al Campanis's *Nightline* appearance, baseball commissioner Peter Ueberroth's office released figures showing that 180 new minority employees had been hired in the previous year, nearly a third of all employees hired during that period. And yet, most of them were instructors, public relations people, special assistants to executives, minor league coaches, trainers, and scouts. During that same year, six teams had replaced managers without hiring a black—Baltimore replaced Cal Ripken, Sr., with Frank Robinson a few weeks later—nine had changed chiefs of operations without hiring a black (Houston hired Bob Watson, a black, as an assistant general manager late in 1988), and baseball history's only black-owned franchise was sold to whites.

At the end of that season, when several teams changed managers—always hiring whites (the most unlikely selection being Doug Rader, who brought a 156-201 record to his new post with the California Angels)—Frank Robinson, speaking from his long-held position as The Only Black Manager, reflected on the post-Campanis era in baseball in an interview with *Baltimore Sun* writer Mike Littwin: "After Campanis, they said, 'Gee, I didn't realize it was that bad. Gee, I hadn't thought about it.' Now they've thought about it, and still nothing has been done."

In 1989, after A. Bartlett Giamatti had been chosen to succeed Ueberroth as baseball's commissioner, a group of National League club owners, led by the Los Angeles Dodgers' Peter O'Malley (the man who had fired Al Campanis), named Bill White, a black man, to replace Giamatti as president of the National League. Only time will tell whether White's historic appointment will defuse or reinforce efforts to increase minority representation in baseball's boardrooms and front offices.

"They tell us to be patient," Frank Robinson said to Littwin. "We've been patient. You still see those things. Lou Piniella, with no experience, is a general manager. Dal Maxvill, same thing. Ted Simmons stops playing and becomes farm director. How long do you have to be patient?"

Post-Campanis blacks seem mainly to have secured the right to have their names reported widely as candidates for management jobs that are subsequently given to whites. "When you discuss a minority for these positions, they always say you don't have experience," mused Robinson. "Experience only seems to matter if you're black."

B L A C K

QUARTERBACKS

"Seven of the starting quarterbacks in the Big Ten were black last season. They are proving they can do the job, so it's just a matter of time before we benefit from this in the NFL."

—BUDDY YOUNG,
FORMER ASSISTANT TO NFL COMMISSIONER PETE ROZELLE, 1974
(WHEN THERE WERE TWO BLACK STARTING QUARTERBACKS IN THE NFL)

"There haven't been too many [black] pure passers. As we get more and more of them in college, we'll see them in the pros."
—NFL COMMISSIONER PETE ROZELLE, 1987
(WHEN THERE WERE THREE)

Carl Sagan, explaining why people need sports, has observed that humans, however technologically advanced, remain emotionally linked to the Pleistocene Era, the brutal period during which humans first appeared. Sagan's thesis may help explain the special appeal of the National Football League, a kingdom of megafauna where clothesline tackles and forearm shivers bring back ancient truths.

Our favorite players, by and large, are those whose behavior seems most primitive—the Bubbas and Butkuses, the Alzados and L.T.'s. There is, however, one exception: We reserve our shining reverence for the leader of the pack. The quarterback, the image of intelligence and maturity, sacrifice and command, is the figure in whom we hope our sons, watching with us, will recognize themselves. The names carry the resonance, the gravity of military commanders. Van Brocklin. Starr. Unitas. Tittle, his pate bleeding, battered in the dust. Staubach. Griese. Hard-drinking Bobby Layne. Elway. Otto Graham. And now—maybe—Doug Williams.

When Doug Williams, by throwing four touchdown passes in perhaps the most perfect big-game quarter a quarterback ever played, led the Washington Redskins to victory in Super Bowl XXII, he demolished several ancient and debilitating stereotypes about the ability of blacks to play the position. Whites clearly listened to him in the huddle. He got hurt and didn't quit. When the Redskins fell behind, the team didn't mutiny under his command. Most of all, he directed his team to a win in the season's biggest game. In one historic evening, Doug Williams kicked a door open. But whether he kicked it down remains to be seen.

In the four decades that blacks have played in the NFL, only nine players have ever thrown more than twenty-five passes, one of them a halfback (Walter Payton). Most black quarterbacks who have played professionally have done so in Canada, or in counter-culture leagues like the USFL or the World Football League. Canada has long been the special sanctuary for the black quarterback: Larry Robertson, statistician for the Canadian Football League, estimates that between fifty and one hundred black Americans have played quarterback in the CFL. The first, an ex–Syracuse University star named Bernie Custis, played in 1951, two years before the first black NFL quarterback appeared. And in the 1988–89 season, there were six black quarterbacks on the eight Canadian team rosters, while in the U.S.—even after Williams's heroics—there were only five black quarterbacks scattered among the NFL's twenty-six teams.

For each of the quarterbacks who got a chance in the NFL—and not always a good chance—scores of other black kids who have wanted to lead, as Keith Lee did, have been told that they are too fast, too athletic, too inexperienced, and that they went to the wrong school.

■

Growing up, Keith Lee was always the quarterback in football and the pitcher in baseball. He had a good arm, and he enjoyed taking the responsibility for what happened in a game. He liked to decide what play to run, what pitch to throw. After he became a high school All-American quarterback in the mid-seventies at Los Angeles's Gardenia High, the world was his. Scholarship offers flooded in from major schools like USC, UCLA, and Texas. The only thing was, none of them wanted him to play quarterback. Apparently his problem was that he was a fast runner. Scouts were not noticing his tactical ability or his inclination to lead. They saw him from the waist down.

He huddled with his father. It had been their dream for Keith to be a college, and then a professional quarterback. "My dad always talked about how important it was for black people to be seen in leadership roles, and to do well," Lee recalls. "I wanted to make him proud."

So he turned down the major schools and enrolled instead at a junior college. There, he figured, he could prove himself as a quarterback and finish as a signal caller for a major university. After Lee's two years as a junior-college All-American quarterback, the scouts came again, from the same big schools, even more this time. But again they wanted him not as quarterback, but as a defensive back, running back, or wide receiver.

Lee enrolled at Colorado State University, whose coaches had recruited him as a quarterback. But when he appeared for the first practice, he discovered he was in competition with two white quarterbacks, both classic, drop-back "pure" passers who ran only as a last resort. Lee could see that once again his coaches were distracted by his ability to run. "When they saw I was black they said, 'Oh, you must be an option quarterback.' I used to get that all the time. I'd say, 'No, I'm not a running quarterback. I'm just a quarterback with the ability to run.' I took it as my chance to prove myself among these so-called quarterbacks who could do nothing else."

One of the quarterback candidates dropped out quickly, and Lee and the other one battled for the starting job throughout the spring and summer. Finally, a week before the first game, Keith Lee got the nod. His dream, and his father's, had come true; the detour into junior college had paid off.

That first game will live forever in Lee's memory. "The other team kicked off to us and we ran it back to the twenty-one. I went over to the coach to get the first play. He gave it to me, and I started to run out to the huddle. Then he grabbed my arm and pulled me back. He said, 'Hey, Keith, why don't you sit this one out? Let Steve go in.' Apparently he had been getting so much pressure from the alumni that he couldn't do it."

Lee didn't play at all that game, and afterward told the coach he was leaving. The following week, when he stopped into the office to say good-bye, the coach relented. "He said, 'Don't leave, we'll put you in at quarterback.' I stayed for two years."

Lee's performance on two mediocre CSU teams was good enough to attract the attention of NFL scouts. But still nothing had changed. One afternoon a Dallas Cowboys scout dropped by the CSU stadium to watch Lee practice. He timed Lee's passes with a radar gun and started to walk away. "Then he said, 'Before I go, why don't you just run a forty?' "

Lee had been expecting this. The 40-yard dash is the legendary Waterloo of black college quarterbacks, the NFL's chance to tell them that they're too fast to stand there and call signals, that something in the defensive backfield, perhaps, might be more suitable. He knew the dream was over. "I ran it, about a four-point-five. He liked it. Then he said, 'Son, have you ever thought about running backwards?' I said, 'Well, not much, just when I'm scrambling,' but he said, 'Let's see you do it.' He timed it. It was fast. That was it."

A few months later the Buffalo Bills drafted Lee as a defensive back. Now a counselor with Northeastern University's Center for the Study of Sport in Society, Lee played for six years in the NFL with Buffalo, New England, and Indianapolis. Perhaps his biggest thrill was at the end. "Indianapolis only carried two quarterbacks my last year," Lee says, "and I got listed as the third quarterback. I never got a snap, but I practiced as a quarterback. When the program came out, with me as a quarterback on it, I sent it to my dad and called him. I said, 'Dad, we made it.' "

■

The first black man ever to take a snap in the NFL was a man named, appropriately, Willie Thrower, who, on October 18, 1953, threw eight passes and completed three for the Chicago Bears against the San Francisco 49ers. Most of them came in one drive when Bears coach George Halas, angry at starting quarterback George Blanda, put Thrower in. Thrower took the Bears from his own 35 to the San Francisco 4-yard line. Then Halas put Blanda back in to score the touchdown. Thrower appeared briefly in two other games that year.

After having been a great college passer at Michigan State, Thrower had hoped to establish himself as Blanda's backup that year, and compete in 1954 for the starting position, but when the Bears' camp opened, he found himself charted as the fourth-string quarterback. "That year," recalls Thrower, who just sold his bar in the Pittsburgh area, "the Bears signed Zeke Bartkowski out of the University of Georgia for seventy-five thousand dollars. It was an unheard-of sum at the time. And they had Ed Brown coming out of the service. They didn't trade players around then. You were in bondage. The handwriting was on the wall for me."

Thrower, like other blacks fleeing bondage before him and many black quarterbacks after him, went to Canada, where he played three happy years in Winnipeg.

While blacks were establishing themselves at all other positions except on the offensive line, the NFL waited nearly a decade to look at a second black quarterback. But they could hardly escape him. In 1961 and 1962, Sandy Stephens, six feet two, 210 pounds, had quarterbacked the University of Minnesota to two successive Rose Bowl appearances, the second time for a victory. He was big, strong, fast, and tough.

In 1962, the Cleveland Browns drafted Stephens in the second round and then traded to him to Detroit, whose coaches greeted him as "the next Paul Hornung." It occurred to Stephens that Paul Hornung was a running back. "Now, I admired Paul Hornung," says Stephens, today a management consultant in the Minneapolis area, "but I wanted a shot at quarterback. I told them I had become first-team All-American, I was fourth in the Heisman voting, above any other quarterback, and I wanted a shot at it, anyway. But they said, 'No, we're already set at that position.' They said I could be a running back and throw the option pass every now and then. It made me feel awful."

So Stephens, too, headed for the eight-team Canadian Football League. "In Canada, they'll give you the opportunity to play quarterback," he explains. "In the NFL, they won't. It's been a thing from way back. Even my parents asked, Why is it we have to go all the way to Canada and play before people who aren't even our own countrymen? And they love you up there. You don't have any problems. In the NFL, blacks aren't supposed to be smart enough to play quarterback. We can run and jump but we can't lead. It's been a perplexing mystery to me. It's stupid."

After two and a half years in Canada, Stephens got one more chance at the NFL, this time with the Kansas City Chiefs, but again, only if he played halfback. He bit. A year later, in 1967, he talked the Chiefs' head coach Hank Stram into giving him a preseason game at quarterback. One tragic play, still well remembered around the NFL, may have doomed him. "I started the first exhibition game of the 1967 season," Stephens recalls. "This was the annual Grocery Bowl, KC against Denver. They had me all wired up so the big radio audience in the Midwest could hear what it sounded like to be in the huddle. In the second half, we were ahead fourteen nothing, and I had driven them about eighty yards, down to the five-yard line.

"I was in the heat of battle now, and down close I always talk to my horses. Before I called the play, I said, 'Now all right, goddammit, let's get that motherfucker *in* there.'" We scored the touchdown and I came joggin' off the field, feeling good, and they said, 'Sandy, Stram wants you up in the press box.' I said sure. I figured he was gonna say, 'Great goin', Sandy.' Instead he said, 'What in the hell are you doing?' Then he told me what happened. That could have had to do with my demise."

Fifteen years after Willie Thrower left the Bears for Canada, a second black stood in under center in the NFL. Midway in the 1968 season, Marlin Briscoe, a college quarterback who had made the Denver Broncos as a defensive back, got a chance to play quarterback when the other quarterbacks got hurt. In his first game he passed for three touchdowns, and he ended up throwing for fourteen in seven games. The next season Briscoe was cut by Denver's new head coach, Lou Saban, who by the 1974 season had at one time or another personally cut four of the five black quarterbacks playing professional football.

In 1970, James Harris became the first black player ever drafted by the NFL to play quarterback, and the first to start for an NFL team. He was six feet three, 221 pounds—pro-quarterback size—and, beyond that, Harris was the product of a deliberate effort by his college coach, Grambling's Eddie Robinson, to deliver an unconvertible black signal-caller to the NFL. "Coach went to New York for a coaches' conference where everyone asked him if he was ever going to produce a black quarterback for the pros," Harris told *The New York Times*. "He took it to heart. After four years I was prepared to compete."

Harris ignored several teams' recommendations that he convert to another position, and was not drafted as a quarterback until the eighth round. Humiliated, he thought about quitting, but Robinson persuaded him to hang on and try to break through. Harris won a job as a part-time starter until Lou Saban took over the Bills in 1971 and cut him outright. "When Saban took over [at Buffalo]" Harris told *Ebony* magazine, "Marlin Briscoe bet me I wouldn't be around much longer, and that year I didn't even get a playbook during the off-season."

Harris waited three years for a second chance. He had given up hope, and was working for the Commerce Department in Washington, D.C., when he was picked up by the Los Angeles Rams. Coach Chuck Knox gave him the time he needed to regain much of his effectiveness, and Harris went on to win twenty of the twenty-four games he started. He was a Pro Bowl quarterback in 1974.

■

Also in 1974, Jefferson Street Joe Gilliam—"Joe Gillie," they called him, as opposed to Joe Willie (Namath)—filled the air with footballs, thirty-yard strings and fifty-yard bombs and eleven-yard bullets thrown half sidearm, off the wrong foot, delivered with a short, cobralike *whap*. His arm action was said to be so quick that even when his Pittsburgh Steeler coaches slowed down the film, his arm remained a blur. He remains a legend in Pittsburgh. "If you ask the guys around here," says Tony Dungy, who recently resigned as the Steelers' defensive coordinator and played on the team from 1977 to 1979, "they'll say he had a better arm, in terms of the mechanics of throwing, than Terry Bradshaw. He was a classic, where you couldn't get around it. You couldn't possibly think of him at any other position."

Tall and razor-thin, he was demonstrably exuberant in a conservative sport's stodgiest period. This was no specialist, looking to keep his job and avoid injury. After a completed pass he pumped his fists in the air. He seemed to prefer come-from-behind wins.

During his tenure as a starting quarterback, which lasted only four preseason games and six regular-season games in 1974, Gilliam lit up the sky. After he took a sulking Terry Bradshaw's job away, *Sports Illustrated* put Gilliam's exultant image on the cover with the self-explanatory title PITTSBURGH'S BLACK QUARTERBACK. *Jet* and *Ebony* ran specials with titles like BLACK QUARTERBACKS: A FOOT IN THE DOOR. Gilliam became Howard Cosell's personal cause, probably alienating many in what became a highly politicized, racially charged struggle for the Steelers' starting-quarterback position.

He was football's Ali. He gave young black football players their first sense that a quarterback role model could be a possibility for them. Keith Lee was a sophomore in high school when Joe Gilliam was ablaze. "I worshiped him," says Lee. "In high school I watched every move he made. I emulated his release. I wore his number—seventeen. I wore my socks like he did, I wore my wristbands like he did. Jefferson Street Joe. I even called myself the Rosecrantz Rifle, because I lived on Rosecrantz Street. When I was in high school he represented hope to me, tangible hope. As a young man, finally I was able to see a black athlete in a leadership role. I saw him direct and coordinate a team of men. Boy, I just admired him. He was my goal."

Joe Gilliam grew up in a football home, surrounded by great

players. His father, Joe Gilliam, Sr., has coached at black colleges in the South for twenty-five years, turning out many NFL stars, most of them defensive giants like Ed "Too Tall" Jones, Jimmy Marsalis, Claude Humphrey, and Waymond Bryant. Joe also developed an early interest in gymnastics and diving. "Until about sixth or seventh grade," says Gilliam, who is now a counselor in the Nashville area, "my interest was doing a double gainer, or a one and a half with a full twist off the three-meter board. I think that helped me take hits later."

Gilliam never played a game at any position but quarterback. Like his father, he had an analytical approach to the game. As a high school player he broke his game into little pieces and then put them back together in games. Over and over, he practiced accelerating the release of his passes, delaying the throw until the last possible instant. In college, he threw sixty-five touchdown passes for his father on three wonderful teams at Tennessee State. He had an inspirational presence in the huddle, and enjoyed improvising at the line. "We had a 'check back' system at Tennessee State," he says, "where I would call the formation in the huddle, and say 'check back.' That meant when we got to the line of scrimmage, and I could see the defense, the next signal would be the play."

Having run a versatile, complex, and pass-oriented offense in college, Gilliam felt well prepared for the NFL. "I had read defenses and called audibles. I had played against great pass rushers that ended up in the pros. I was prepared to play pro ball."

Even though his uncle Frank was head of scouting for the Minnesota Vikings, Gilliam was not picked until the eleventh round of the 1972 NFL draft, the 272nd pick overall. In the Steelers' training camp, however, he did not behave like the standard 272nd pick. For one thing, he refused to show them exactly how fast he could run. While thumbs froze over stopwatches, Gilliam jogged his way through the 40-yard dash. "I might have run an eight flat," he recalls. "They knew what I was doing."

Then, when he made the team, he insisted on the chance to lead. "One of the stipulations in my contract was that they at least had to give me the opportunity to play quarterback. I felt there was no telling what they might try to do to me. There hadn't been any [black] quarterbacks before me that had gotten a heck of a shot. My father had had guys like Roy Curry and Eldridge Dickey. I had seen quarterbacks in the late fifties and early sixties that those guys in the pros couldn't even compete with. There was no comparison. I *was* a quarterback. If I was gonna be a football player, I was a quarterback. If I couldn't have been a quarterback, I would have gone to law school or medical school."

For two years, Gilliam played on the Steelers' specialty teams, a man without a uniform, burning for a chance to play, listed third behind Terry Bradshaw and Terry Hanratty. Then, in the preseason of 1974, he got his chance. He started all four preseason games and shredded every defense, passing for nearly four touchdowns and three hundred yards per game, all of them wins. "After what Joe did in preseason," Steelers coach Chuck Noll told the sporting world, "he deserves to start."

He lasted six games. The Steelers won four of them, and tied another, but fans clamored for his removal. After six games, he had thrown and completed far more passes than any other quarterback in the NFL, but for only four touchdowns. The Steelers' offense was inconsistent—they once went nine quarters without scoring a touchdown—but potent, after the six games ranking sixth in points scored among the twenty-seven teams in the league. But most important, the Steelers were in first place in their division.

Gilliam seemed to realize his only chance was to try to keep some balance, not to press, to view himself not as a symbol, but as a quarterback. But with Bradshaw and Hanratty in the wings, and the whole town into it, at a time when his car was vandalized, when hate mail and menacing phone calls were commonplace, finding a calm center couldn't have been easy. "I don't intend on doing any losing," he told *Ebony* at the time, " 'cause I know it won't take much."

Before the seventh game, against Atlanta, another Monday-night showcase with Howard and Frank and Dandy, Noll told Gilliam that the end had come. Bradshaw was the new quarterback. " 'It's time for a change,' he said," recalls Gilliam. "I have nothing but great things to say about Chuck Noll. He stood by me. I watched him every week defend why he was playing me in front of the press. The only reason I hated it was that Atlanta's defense was so predictable. I was planning on throwin' five or six TDs to beef up my stats against them."

Gilliam, who had won eight of the ten games he started and tied another, never started again for the Steelers, or for any other NFL team. By the time he was traded in 1978 to the New Orleans Saints and released soon after, Gilliam was on his way to a drug addiction that, unfortunately, marks his record for many fans. The Steelers, behind Bradshaw, went on to win the Super Bowl in the 1974–75 season, and three others. If the rapturous Joe Gilliam had been the one throwing those Super Bowl bombs to Stallworth and Swann, and slugging the ball into Franco's gut, the barriers for black quarterbacks might be distant memories by now. And maybe not.

Asked what he thinks his experience meant to young quarterbacks, Gilliam speaks softly. "I guess the fact that I left under such dubious circumstances, with drugs and all, didn't help. But they saw a black man call his own plays and handle his own game plan and win football games."

■

Even though in 1978 Warren Moon was voted the PAC-Eight player of the year and led his college team to an upset Rose Bowl victory, and even though at six feet three and 210 pounds he had the physical stature the NFL seeks in a quarterback, Moon simply assumed after college that the NFL would not take him seriously as a quarterback (he was right—he wasn't drafted). He signed with the Edmonton Eskimos of the Canadian Football League instead and became an instant legend. In his six seasons in Canada, he led the team to five league championships and twice passed for more single-season yardage than any quarterback in the history of professional football. By the end, Moon ranked with Wayne Gretzky and Ann Murray in the hearts of Canadians.

In 1984, when Moon's contract expired, he simply announced to the football world that he was available. In all, fourteen teams in the NFL, Canadian Football League, and the United States Football League mounted one of the most frenzied pursuits in the history of professional sports, which Moon ended by signing a $6 million contract with Houston. It took several years for Moon to become established as a first-rank NFL quarterback. In his first years he was notable mainly for throwing interceptions, but by the 1987–88 season, he had led the Oilers to the AFC championship game, and in the next season became a Pro Bowler.

Moon's package sent a signal that it was possible for a black quarterback to be rewarded seriously. "He [Moon] is in a different category than the rest of us," said Doug Williams in a 1987 interview with the Cleveland *Plain Dealer.* "He got his money up front. For people like Randall Cunningham and [Dallas's] Reggie Collier, it's a different ball game. We work from year to year, hoping we got a job. We do slave wages compared to a lot of NFL quarterbacks. Cunningham is a starter, and he'll only be making around $200,000. [In July 1988, Randall Cunningham signed a multimillion-dollar contract that made him the highest-paid player on the Eagles' team.] Cunningham's backup [Matt Cavanaugh, who is white] is making around $500,000. Now I'm not all that good in addition and subtraction, but my God!" Williams, a ten-year veteran who led an underpowered Tampa Bay team to the play-offs three times in his five seasons with the team, might have noted that he, too, made less than Cavanaugh in 1987.

■

If Moon is the first black quarterback to get rich, and Doug Williams the first to win big, some think Philadelphia's Randall Cunningham may end up scoring an even bigger breakthrough. After three seasons as a starting quarterback for the Philadelphia Eagles, his ability to run has not been held against him. In fact it seems to be counted as an asset. There are plays in the Eagles' offense that *require* Cunningham to run, not as a last resort, or as a half-yard sneak, but from anywhere on the field, because the coaching staff considers him likely to advance the football with his feet. In the 1988–89 season he accounted for nearly 80 percent of Philadelphia's offense and was named in one poll the NFL's outstanding player. If Cunningham could pass and run the Eagles into the Super Bowl, he could become the prototype signal-caller of the nineties, an active, multidimensional weapon who could make today's tall, wide-hipped, stationary quarterbacks seem obsolete.

■

Still, many football coaches and scouts contend that most black quarterbacks leave college unprepared to grasp the high-tech, pass-dominated offenses found in the NFL. In this view, almost all black applicants went to the wrong college; either their coaches made them run too much to develop as passers, or, if they were passers, the school they went to was too small or rural to give them a serious technical education. "The tendency is still to look at him [the black quarterback] more as a runner than a passer," Dallas coach Tom Landry explained to *The New York Times* in 1987. "The trend is still toward using the drop-back quarterback. We're still not in the position in the NFL where the running quarterback can be a dominant factor."

Leo Cahill, for twenty years a scout, coach, and general manager in the Canadian Football League and now the general manager of the Toronto Argonauts, agrees with Landry. "What's happened is they spend so much time at a school like Oklahoma or Nebraska or Houston, working on that option play—take the ball away, hand it, keep it, pitch it off—that they don't have the time to spend on the drop-back passing game. The colleges in the States take a kid who is a great running back, and because of his running ability, they've made a quarterback out of him. Some of these kids can throw pretty good but they don't learn to read defenses and pick out receivers. Fresh out of college there's no way they are ready for a professional-style, drop-back passing game."

Couldn't they learn? Cahill is asked. Don't NFL teams keep white journeymen, apprentices who sooner or later get a chance? And who calls his own plays anymore, anyway? (In 1987, among twenty-eight quarterbacks, only New England's Grogan and Pittsburgh's Mark Malone did so; the others received signals from a player on the sidelines who in turn got them from a coach in the press box.) Impatience enters Cahill's voice. "Look, the only way that you can understand what I'm talking about is if you've had a background in football. You need a student of the game to play quarterback. I'm talking about a guy who's been groomed to be a drop-back quarterback. There's such a small time when it's put up or shut up in training camp that you can't keep a guy around and groom him when you've got other guys who are ahead of him. In the NFL, many are called but few are chosen."

Tony Dungy, who, as defensive coordinator of the Cleveland Browns, is the highest-ranking black NFL coach, offers an alternative analysis. Dungy was a highly successful college quarterback at the University of Minnesota, but like so many other black signal-callers, was not offered a chance to play quarterback in the NFL. He found himself having to choose between a quarterback offer in Canada and a chance to play defensive back in the NFL. "They [the NFL] said I was too short," Dungy recalls, chuckling. "I was six feet tall. I had met Bob Griese and looked in his eye, and Fran Tarkenton and looked *above* him. Still, I was too short."

Dungy thinks black quarterback candidates are victims of a double standard. "In the NFL a quarterback is supposed to be between six-two and six-four with a very strong arm," he says. "Now, if you don't have that, then you're supposed to have the 'intangibles,' the 'necessities,' like Griese or Tarkington or Flutie or Billy Kilmer. My contention would be that if a black quarterback doesn't fit the prototype, we don't ever get a chance to look at his intangibles. Then they say, 'Well, he's a good athlete—he could play another position.'

"If a white quarterback doesn't fit the prototype, you say, 'Yeah, but he's smart' or 'a leader' or 'has good timing.' You *look* for redeeming qualities, and a lot of these players end up being the stars, the Bart Starrs, Johnny Unitases, the Bob Grieses. With the black quarterback, either we try him at another position or we write him off and say he can't do it at all. I don't think we ever say about the black quarterback, 'Well, he doesn't have exactly what we're looking for, but what *does* he have?' We haven't seen too many backup, second-team, journeymen black quarterbacks."

Ask football men what it takes to be a good quarterback and their voices drop to a tone of reverence. And the answers are usually not about great gifts, but about intangibles. They describe the short, slow, shrewd, and gutty men who traditionally have been the NFL's best quarterbacks. "I've seen some great throwers and intelligent kids," says Cahill, "but that's not the main thing. I say to be a quarterback you gotta be able to get in a huddle and tell ten guys a story and they all gotta believe you."

"I don't really think there are any necessities," says Tony Dungy. "The necessity is that you can be a winner. Guys like Joe Kapp and Billy Kilmer, they weren't poetic, but they won. More guys like that end up being more successful than the guy who's drafted number one. Mainly you need a chance to develop."

■

The door to the football hero's job may or may not be opening, but there is no doubt that there are more applicants now than ever waiting outside in the lobby. In the 1987–88 season, 26 of the 105 NCAA Division 1-A college-football teams started a black quarterback during at least part of the season. And there are reports of scores of black high school quarterbacks behind them, being schooled not to run, but to stay in the pocket and slide delicately for first downs and look tall.

Still, there have been times like this before; in 1974, seven of the ten starting quarterbacks in the Big Ten conference were black, a phenomenon that made many believe that prosperity was just around the corner.

Probably most black NFL quarterback candidates will continue to be branded too fast, too athletic, and too inexperienced until there are black head coaches and offensive coordinators. The only black who has ever been head coach of a major professional football team did so—predictably—in the Canadian Football League (ex–Green Bay Packer star Willie Wood, who coached the Toronto Argonauts in 1980–81). "To be a good quarterback your personality has to fuse with that of your coach," says Sandy Stephens. "You have to end up thinking with one mind. You spend your time together, watching films together at somebody's house. You have to get to know your coach."

"On most [NFL] staffs, there is maybe one black coach," Tony Dungy explains. "It seems like most organizations have said, 'We gotta get one, as long as we do that, we're OK.' Owners in our league really want to win. They'll do anything to get a competitive advantage. Most of our owners are not football men. They won't be able to look at the coaching staff and say, 'Boy, whoever coaches the running backs must be a good coach.' They have to go by the media and word of mouth. If John Madden says on TV, 'Here's the next young great coach,' he gets hot. I don't think it's structured to keep anyone out, but our owners really don't know who the good coaches are."

Some black quarterbacks have come to feel that they have been held down less by their training or size or speed than by the simple notion that white people are less likely to pay money to see black people lead football teams. "Network sponsorship and ticket sales, not winning, generates money," says Keith Lee. "The predominant fan that attends the game is white and middle class with children. It's far more appealing [to them] to identify with a player in the heroic role if it's a white guy."

Canadians marvel at this idea. "It's such a volatile issue," says David Watkins, information director for the Toronto Argonauts, a team whose 1987 roster included, at various times, three American black quarterbacks, none of whom was drafted to play quarterback by the NFL. "There's innuendo up here about what goes on down in the NFL. When Willie Totten came up here [after not being drafted by the NFL], our coach said, 'Don't put me on the record but I think what they say about the NFL is true. They just don't feel that a black quarterback is marketable.' "

Black or white, only those who have been quarterbacks can really know what it means to stand under center, clean and erect, pointing and shouting and directing, while everyone else either looks toward or crouches beneath you. ABC sportscaster Frank Gifford, a star college quarterback with Hollywood looks, was converted to halfback as a professional. He never got over it.

Gifford told columnist Bob Greene in a book titled *Cheeseburgers* that with one exception, there hasn't been anything in his life that he hasn't been able to get. Money, jobs, respect, the admiration of beautiful women—those things came easily. No, he said, it was something else, something that spoke to his very essence. Gifford's frustration is something that many black football players since Willie Thrower's time, players who have found themselves sidetracked to Canada, waylaid in defensive backfields, or lining up far to the side of the ball, could understand. "Look, I don't want you to get the idea that I dwell on this," Gifford told Greene. "But always, in my own mind I was a quarterback. I was never a halfback. I didn't *want* to be a quarterback. I *was* a quarterback. Nobody ever seemed to understand that."

4

BUOYANCY:
WHY FEW
BLACKS
SWIM
IN THE
OLYMPICS

I n 1844, the Swimming Society in England invited a group of Native Americans to swim in an exhibition. Their American contacts had reported observing them swimming with considerable speed, using an outlandish technique that simply had to be seen. The featured event in the exhibition was a race between two Native Americans named Flying Gull and Tobacco. At the command, they dived in, and, as predicted, propelled themselves through the water in a way that amazed and offended Londoners. One scandalized observer reported that they "thrashed the water violently with their arms, like sails of a windmill, and beat downward with their feet, blowing with force and forming grotesque antics." It was, reported the swim club in the most damning epithet the writer could summon, "totally un-European."

It was also Europe's introduction to the crawl, the foundation of modern competitive swimming, the stroke by which West Africans and Native Americans and some Pacific Islanders had been transporting themselves through water for centuries. In fact, Anglo domination of swimming has been a fairly recent phenomenon. Until early in the century, the best Australian swimmers were dark-skinned Solomon Islanders. Hawaiians flatly dominated U.S. Olympic teams, for which they swam between 1912 and 1952. Several Hawaiian competitors—including the best, Duke Kahanamoku, a man who later played silent Polynesians, Hindus, and Native Americans in more than a hundred films, had very dark skin. "The dark-skinned Hawaiians did a great deal to break the color line in America thirty years before Jackie Robinson," wrote Buck Dawson, the president of the International Swimming Hall of Fame, in his history of American swimming *From Weissmuller to Spitz.*

Whites who have developed a grudging willingness to share mongrel diversions like baseball, football, and basketball have thrown their shoulders against the gates of private country clubs, places where people get good at pursuits like tennis and golf and team swimming. As late as 1975, long after other sports had at least allowed token quantities of blacks in the door and allowed them to play reactive positions, the Masters Golf Tournament refused to invite blacks to participate (even though almost all the caddies were black). When asked why, the tournament's long-standing czar, Clifford Roberts, would reply that no black had ever proved himself good enough to warrant an invitation—this despite the steady accomplishments of North Carolinian Charlie Sifford, whose first PGA win had come in 1967 and who had been in the PGA's top sixty every year between 1960 and 1969.

Whites have been least willing to mix with blacks in water. Throughout much of this century, laws and ordinances kept blacks out of public pools. Where there were no laws, many whites became uncomfortable or fearful if blacks dared to enter, as if the blackness itself would ooze off into the water. "People thought some pretty weird things," recalls Buck Dawson. "I can remember going places where they said you had to change the water in the pool if a black swam in it."

The Olympic Games presents the only real showcase for competitive swimming, and no American black has ever made the U.S. Olympic team. Suriname's Anthony Nesty—who trained in the United States—won a gold medal in the 1988 Olympics, and Holland's Enith Brigitha won two bronze medals in the 1976 games. There have been, through the decades, a few black college champions, but the closest any American black has come to the spotlight is when UCLA freestyler Chris Silva missed making the 1984 U.S. squad by about half a second.

Whites have long been content to explain the scarcity of black swimming champions by supposing the entire race to be defective in water. South African Olympic chief Frank Braun concluded in 1968 that blacks didn't make South African teams because water clogged the pores of their skin. "There was a theory," recalls Buck Dawson, "that blacks had thicker skulls than whites. There was one about their ankles being inflexible too. Everyone called them 'sinkers.' "

To say that a group can't swim is hardly the same as saying that its members can't serve or putt or volley. It is rather to assert that they are incomplete, lacking the competence to function in one of earth's basic elements. The hypothesis that blacks have greater difficulty in water than whites is scientifically unsupported, in no small part because the topic's sensitivity has discouraged research. "I myself was once interested in the theory that heavier skulls kept blacks out of swimming," recalls Buck Dawson. "But it sounded like a racist remark so I couldn't pursue it."

Ironically, those same "fixed" ankles, once regarded as anchors that kept blacks from kicking freely, are now hailed as an asset by some. "Within six years after the first black makes the Olympic team, I would say that all sprints, anything from the two hundred [meters] on down in all strokes will be won by blacks," says Jane Stafford, who has since 1968 coached the Capital Sea Devils, a racially mixed team of Washington, D.C.–based swimmers, and who is white. "That's because their ankles aren't fastened the same. So they get this terrific leap [off the blocks] just like Dr. J. in basketball."

Hearing for centuries that they are designed to drown has kept centuries of black people from entering water over their heads. For many of them, water is something to splash in, not to swim in, and certainly not to race in. "Black kids still use that 'we can't' as an excuse not to get in deep water," says Stafford. "But I realize now that the problem isn't that they're sinkers. I coached one white NCAA champion who would sink like a stone if he tried to float. With blacks, it's because they're programmed for failure from the time they're five years old. They're told they can't do it. And when you tell any kid they can't, they won't. I have had ten or twelve kids over the years who have had the ability to make the U.S. Olympic team. They'll break records in practice, but put them in with white kids and it's like they have an anchor and chains. They think whites hate them from the start."

America's few black collegiate champion swimmers have had to displace a great deal more than chlorinated water to make their marks. Chris Silva, the first black U.S. swimmer to set an American record (as a member of the UCLA 400-yard freestyle relay team in 1983) and a silver medalist in the 1983 World Games, learned about his supposed deficiencies as a five-year-old. He had first tasted chlorine the year before, when his father, a navy captain, tossed him off the diving board at the YMCA pool near their home in Menlo Park, California. This was hardly an act of cruelty. It was a way to end the kid's incessant nagging to go swimming. Thrilled, Chris surfaced, paddled to the side, and asked his dad to do it again.

He started lessons at the Y the next Monday. It pleased his mother, Dessie, to think that swimming was available to her son. As a girl, she hadn't been allowed to swim in public pools. Besides, the lessons didn't cost much. Before long, Chris was competing, and winning, on the Y team.

Then one day, when Chris was five, the Y's athletic director asked Dessie Silva if she and Chris would go with him to Long Beach, Washington, for a clinic. It was over a day's drive, and Chris was ill, but the official insisted. It would be good for the Y, he said, and it would help Chris learn his kick turns.

When they got there, they discovered that Chris himself was to be the centerpiece of the clinic. The boy was exhibited as a specimen, that rarity the Negro swimmer. "This man described to everyone about the texture of the hair of black people," Dessie Silva recalls. "He said Chris had heavy bones, and that that was the cause of us not being able to swim."

She removed Chris from the Y program and got him into the first of a string of expensive country clubs, but they never could escape the sense of their own novelty—Chris can remember competing against only one other black swimmer before he entered college—or the sense that others were trying to discourage them. "It came up again and again," Dessie Silva says. "They said we couldn't float, that the oil from our skin was a problem . . . at this point, I would just like to forget all those things. I get to talking about them and I get angry. Prejudice is there. Once you go through it, it either makes you what they say you are—a quitter, someone who's too dumb to learn—or you will go on and set your mind to it and just do it."

■

Why has there never been a black U.S. Olympic swimmer? The answer lies in knowing what it takes to be a swimming champion, namely, an Olympic-size pool available to you at all hours, some way to get to it and home, a skilled, encouraging, and usually manipulative coach, enough food to replace thousands of burned calories, a checkbook big enough to pay for lodging, food, transportation to meets, and a surprising array of equipment, and, crucially, a capacity to endure the tedium of spending much of your time in a chlorine-filled pool with your face in the water.

Many blacks have no water to swim in in their neighborhoods. While it costs very little public money to finance a strip of asphalt and a couple of netless rims, investing in an Olympic-size pool is another matter. American blacks have had access mainly to crowded, dirty, ill-maintained, and undersize public pools. Most inner-city high schools do not have pools.

Not that all great swimmers have come from Olympic-size pools. Many of the great Hawaiians were trained in an irrigation ditch by a visionary coach, Soichi Sakamoto, who, standing above them with a metronome, gave them concepts of rhythm and pace. When they climbed out of the ditch, he would tell them things like "The light of success comes only when everything seems hopeless and wasted."

But blacks have had no Sakamoto. They have received little support and almost no technical training, for there are few whites who want to spend their time cultivating black swimmers in tough neighborhoods, and, so far, few black coaches who know how to produce swimming champions. Maybe most important of all, it is safe to say that most black kids have never seen a good black competitive swimmer to imitate. "Brown tries to recruit blacks," says Brown University swimming coach Ed Reed. "But swimming tends to attract middle-class kids. "You don't have the exposure to swimming programs in the ghetto. They [blacks] look to popular media sports instead. You can't get a three-million-dollar contract as a rookie swimmer. Where in the hell are they even gonna find a pool in the Northeast?"

Good competitive swimmers need to swim almost constantly, and, like golfers and tennis players who require sponsorship, it takes a lot of someone's time, patience, and money to keep them in a pool. Black football and basketball players often come from homes bound together by a single, exhausted woman, but given the financial and logistical demands of top-flight, competitive swimming, it is almost impossible for a working single parent to raise a swimming champion.

Barbara Davis, the divorced mother of national high school freestyle champion Byron Davis, who is black, remembers what it was like to support a teenage swimmer while working at two hospitals as a practical nurse, studying at night to become a registered nurse, and raising another child with demanding interests. "There were a lot of times when I had to work all night, go home, toot the horn, and he'd jump in and we'd be off to Willoughby or Youngstown or somewhere. Then, once we'd get there, I would take my blanket and go somewhere and sleep or study. The other parents would come and get me when Byron was ready to swim. We did that for quite a few years."

The expense is surprising. At a typical meet involving travel, there are stiff entry fees, transportation, food, and lodging costs, not to mention equipment costs—goggles, earplugs, chlorine-removing shampoos, three or four sets of trunks and sweats. "It is terribly, terribly expensive," says Dessie Silva. "We had to be willing to make sacrifices beyond all imagination. When Chris stopped swimming it saved, like, ninety dollars a month for me plus three hundred dollars assessed fees a year. He had reached a level where he could go to a three-day meet and swim five events a day. That's a dollar and a half an event. He would have to have somewhere to stay. He would have to have food, and gas. When it comes to swimming, money is the number-one thing."

And of course, swimmers are developed as teenagers. The average black teenager is more likely than a white counterpart to have been raised by one parent, to be a parent, to be out of work, and to be exposed to the minefield of drugs and disease and violence that are tragic features of contemporary urban life. Washington, D.C.'s Capital Sea Devils have only three rules, rules that they post on their bulletin board and encourage each other to obey. They are:

1. No making babies on the team's time.
2. No drugs or alcohol.
3. We help each other.

According to the United States Swimming office, there are today about twenty-five hundred competitive swim clubs in the United States, about four hundred of which are capable of producing an Olympian. The private club is the foundation of American competitive swimming. It consists typically of a team, a paid coach, a home pool, a weight room, and a group of dues-paying members, who, because swimming is a voracious consumer of time, are together a great deal. So far, at least, almost all of America's fast backstrokers and freestylers have been white suburban club-members whose parents have given over their calendars and checkbooks to dawn practices, vitamin supplements, and weekend meets.

A few clubs, mainly in California and Florida, where swimmers can compete outdoors all year round, have produced a disproportionate share of champions. The members-only country club can present an almost tribal cliquishness, a palpable cohesion that is daunting even for white newcomers and has not been easy for black pioneers to penetrate. "California is terrible," says Dessie Silva. "They will grin in your face and then get behind your back and it's just the opposite. If they're alone with you they'll be friendly but if they get with their group they'll give you hell. But I don't believe in 'staying where you belong.' It's a free world—at least they keep tellin' me that."

Membership in one private Florida club, an institution whose practice lanes are jammed with ex–Olympic medalists, entitles one to the privileges of what its brochure describes as "a total lifestyle." The Mission Bay Swim Club, centerpiece of a 565-acre planned residential community in Boca Raton, Florida (whose "private islands of luxury" peak at around a third of a million dollars), offers those who can afford it a gold card to a Brave New World of blood-chemistry testing, underwater photography, and computerized stroke-modeling.

As Mark Schubert, coach of the Mission Bay Makos swim team—a man who twice coached the men's U.S. Olympic team— says in promotional literature, "Mission Bay can take a child from preschool lessons through local, national and international competition and to the master's program." All for around $1,000 a year per family member in fees. After Montessori classes, Mission Bay's preschool swimmers can plunge from stainless-steel starting blocks into one of four pools whose water is maintained constantly at a temperature of 88 degrees. They flail along between official Keifer competitor lane lines, while the Colorado time system— which includes a dot-matrix scoreboard—records their time. And, as they mature, when a loss becomes unendurable or a plateau too stressful, sports psychologist Dr. Don Greene, who "conducted the only research study in existence which tested and improved S.W.A.T. officers' performance under extreme stress," is right there for them at poolside.

By contrast, in most major cities there is at least one inner-city swim team that includes some black swimmers. Sometimes the team is built around a YMCA pool—like the team from the Patton Pool in Detroit, which has produced highly competitive black swimmers since the forties—while others operate with some form of public assistance, like the Capital Sea Devils, which uses facilities provided by the Department of Defense.

There is, in metropolitan Cleveland, an example of what amounts to an inner-city country club. Since 1980, the Cleveland Barracudas Swim Club, a team of twenty-five black boys and girls from seven to eighteen years of age, has been part of the Lake Erie League, whose other, nearly all-white teams are scattered throughout the city's thirty-five suburbs. The Barracudas Swim Club is a squad backed not by sports psychologists and family vans but by single mothers—only one of the swimmers has a father living in the household—and bus passes. Most of all it is supported by the giant heart of its coach.

Clarence E. "Moby" McLeod III, a black, thirty-nine-year-old ex-backstroker, has been trying to mold black competitive swimmers for twenty years. He coaches for free because he knows no one can afford to pay him. Unmarried, he lives with his parents, pays for too many of his swimmers' expenses out of a tow-truck driver's shallow pocket, and, to keep them going, has put his own education on a rather indefinite hold.

When asked why he does it, he answers by asking why more people don't. "No one has wanted to take the time with them," he says. "There is all the peer pressure, the drugs, the pornography. Without someone besides their parents and grandparents to help them, I can see some of them not making it to their eighteenth birthday, or the girls not making it to twenty-one without having children. I try to raise these kids to be young adults. My parents did for me."

Despite their poverty, Moby McLeod is, like Mission Bay's

Mark Schubert, trying to develop champions. "All my life I've heard that black people couldn't swim," he says, "and I've been determined to prove they are wrong. My goal is to coach at least one kid who can make it to the Olympics someday."

Whenever he and the mothers can afford it, he enters his kids in meets that, for now, they have little chance to win, out in the suburbs with the good swimmers in superior pools. He does so because he wants his swimmers to overcome the sense that they are exotic, unwelcome, and most of all, undeserving. He feels they can't win until they believe they have a right to be in any and every pool. Even though they'll feel more at home collecting medals and ribbons against the inner-city YMCA teams, they won't improve. If we're ever gonna be good, he tells them, we're gonna have to be good out in Lakewood and Shaker Heights, out with the good white swimmers.

■

On a July afternoon, Barracuda practice starts when the strongest kids can make enough noise on the pool door to wake their coach from his nap. Moby drove the truck last night from midnight till seven, running out to I-90 to take care of stranded Triple A members, changing their spares and jumpstarting their engines, hauling them in as a last resort, impounding cars for the police in between runs. The night held nothing unusual—nothing especially grisly, no one to pry out, but busy enough to keep him from catching any sleep between runs. Then, as usual, he was at the Cuyahoga Community College pool at eight for the children's morning program, followed by the college beginners at eleven, the afternoon children from one to three, and, at last, a nap until the fists on the door got too loud.

Clad in his standard yellow Barracuda coach's T-shirt, trunks, and sandals, Moby pads over and opens the door, rubbing his eyes.

He is an immense man with a light reddish Afro and a formidable belly long ago weakened by a robber's bullet and long since stretched by too many gallon-size Pepsis. His is the bearing of a sumo.

The kids stream past him, slapping down their weekly book reports on a poolside table, and begin to lay out kickboards and hook up long beaded ropes to form eight lanes across the pool. The girls wear their hair in cornrows, fixed tightly with bright beads to reduce water drag. Somehow, almost all the boys are wearing designer athletic shoes, Reeboks and Air Jordans and Avias.

They peel to their official blue Barracuda team-member T-shirts and swimsuits for calisthenics. Nine of the boys and girls have shirts with the initials "E.F." on the breast. That stands for "elite force," Moby's core, the S.W.A.T. team, the few, the proud, the fast.

Moby sinks down at the practice table and toys with a stop-watch as an eighteen-year-old backstroker named Stacey Mitchell leads them through an impressive regimen of calisthenics, rope exercises, and agility drills. They have free access to the college pool—or the Tri-C, as everyone calls it—three evenings a week and on Saturday mornings. Without that singular blessing—Moby estimates it would cost $500 a month to rent a pool—the Barracudas could not exist. The other Lake Erie League teams, which have their own pools, are able to swim more, and so the Barracudas try to keep up by working hard every practice.

Out of their earshot, Moby loves to talk about his swimmers. He has taught all but one to swim, from blowing bubbles to the four strokes. He pulls up his shirt and displays a set of parallel tracks along his middle back. "Yaz put that there," he says, pointing out a tiny girl who looks to be maybe nine. "Her mother brought her in here saying that the preacher couldn't even get her head under water to baptize her. She was that scared of getting her head wet. One night I picked her up and kind of dangled her off the diving board. She dug into me pretty good."

Moby first meets his swimmers when, like Yaz, they walk into the Tri-C—with their mothers, some of whom take classes at the college. They hear about his beginners' swimming class and ask him if he can keep their kids from drowning. Usually he ends up teaching the mothers too. He knows that some of them, on meeting him, size him up as a surrogate father—a combination authority figure and baby-sitter. That's fine with him, as long as they'll support the team—show up to meets and practices, pay the $10-a-month-per-kid dues and not give in to the kids when they complain that swimming is hard.

Clyde Briscoe, a fourteen-year-old butterflyer who is without speech or hearing, came to Moby three years ago with his brother Charles. Deafness, Moby discovered, presents special problems for swimmers. "Clyde can't hear the starter's commands in a race. At first he always started behind the others. We tried waving at him, but nothing worked. Then one practice his brother whacked him on the rear at the start. Now we have a designated tapper for Clyde at every meet." They communicate with Clyde through a Barracuda sign language, a homegrown patois of universal and local gestures. Moby illustrates with a snapping down of fisted hands held together. "This means I'll break his neck if he doesn't beat his brother," he explains.

Moby believes devoutly in two things: education and push-ups. He thinks that black kids run too much and develop relatively little upper-body strength. Thus the push-up has become his universal currency. Miss your weekly Barracuda book report and it's a hundred on the spot. Miss a flash card while he's helping you with math and it's twenty. Race him through a set of flash cards, and he'll do twenty if he loses. Cross him, or disappoint him, and you will get to know the feel of the Tri-C's cool tile floor.

The typical Barracuda reports for practice hungry and with no way home. Moby taxis them in a gray van—donated, like the pool time, by the Tri-C—to keep them off the buses late at night. He usually ends up buying them a snack too. He sermonizes constantly to the kids and their parents about nutrition, exhorting them to spend food money on granola bars, not fries, to drink milk instead of soda. His grandest contempt is for the Cleveland public-school menu. "A lot of 'em throw breakfast away because it's that bad," he says with disgust. "Lunch is the same way. Then they'll come home and grab a peanut butter sandwich and come over here and try to do a workout of four or five thousand yards on that."

Moby's older swimmers, like Michael Mais and Clyde Briscoe, go to Cleveland's public high schools. They want badly to swim all year round, if for no other reason so they won't fall further behind their Lake Erie League counterparts who swim for their high school teams in the heated, Olympic-size pools of Cleveland's suburbs. Moby has offered to coach them himself during the school year, free of charge, using the Tri-C pool for training. All he asks, he tells their athletic directors, is for the school to let the kids wear the schools' colors and compete in interscholastic meets. They say they'll get back to him. Mostly, if they do, they end up telling him about liability insurance.

■

As calisthenics end and workouts begin, a few parents and friends begin to straggle in after work to watch practice. Each swimmer follows a carefully tailored workout, and every kid has times to meet, teammates to beat, scores to settle and meets for which to qualify.

Stacey Mitchell, who got the Barracudas started in 1980 by

asking Moby if he would coach a group of her siblings and friends, is trying to win a spot on the Cleveland State University swim team. An athletic scholarship would show the mothers and their skeptical boyfriends that there is money in swimming—maybe not like an NBA contract, but something worth having and within reach. Michael Mais and Marcus Johnson, powerful fourteen-year-old breaststrokers, want at each other. Sandra Moore is going for thirty-eight seconds in the 50 free, Tracy Mais for fifty-four in the 100 free. Roberto Cottingham, having already beaten Arthur Wilson in practice, is out after Charles Briscoe. Charles Briscoe mainly wants to join his girlfriend Cartrina Moore on the "elite force," so everyone will stop razzing him.

Moby prowls the pool's edge, dishing out incentives, pouring kerosene on competitive fires, threatening push-ups. Needling, he sets up a "grudge" match between Clyde and Charles. "Someone tell Clyde if he loses it's a hundred push-ups," Moby yells. Moby blows the whistle, someone slaps Clyde on the butt, and the water is instant froth. As the two boys churn back and forth, one of the parents happens to remark that she doesn't think there is a single person, parent or child, in the entire room that Moby hasn't taught to swim. Everyone looks around. It's true.

Moby thinks he's taught about three thousand people to swim, almost all of them black, most of them in the Tri-C pool. The parents say that once you've been underwater with Moby, convinced that your life is in his hands, it's hard to let him down later when he asks for your help. He has been able to help them overcome a fear of deep water that began when they were children. "I remember I was standing by a lake," says Don Stewart, Moby's former assistant, "back when I was in college, watching this white kid swim. Right when I was standing there the kid got in trouble. His father went right in there after him and saved him. I remember thinking, 'I couldn't do that for *my* kid.' Then, when

I got back to college, I had Moby teach me to swim, and then he taught my kids."

Josie Mais, grandmother of two Barracudas, says that growing up in Alabama she had always heard that blacks had blood that got colder in cold water. At first she had been concerned for this reason that her grandchildren would catch colds in the winter if she let them swim. She took Moby's beginners' swimming class at the Tri-C when she was in her sixties, fearful, like those she had grown up with, of deep water. On the day of reckoning, when it was time to jump into water over her head, she hung back in the shallow end. Moby swam over and asked her why. Lowering her eyes, she revealed that she wasn't buoyant. At the time she weighed nearly three hundred pounds. Moby challenged her at least to find out for herself.

Josie Mais was hardly a quitter. She was a woman who, without help, had raised seven children, none of them her own, all placed on her doorstep by others in various forms of trouble. "I don't care what happened before," she told each kid after the parent left, "from here on you go forward."

She decided to plunge. "I put my feet on top of his and we held on to each other and jumped in," she says, shaking her head. "We went all the way to the bottom, with our toes locked. Then he let me go and I came up first. Then I knew."

Phyllis Moore, the twenty-seven-year-old mother of Warren, ten, Cartrina, twelve, and Sandra, twelve, walks in and slumps into a chair. Today, she announces, has been a flat-out lousy day. She has been trying for weeks to get a raise at the J. C. Penney store where she works as a manicurist. Today she hit a brick wall. "I told them I need more money," she says. "They said, 'If you don't like what's happening, you can always leave.' I can't leave. I'm just living from paycheck to paycheck."

Smiles surface easily in Phyllis's round face. She is a dedicated but tired parent, a young woman who has raised three children by herself. She lives in her mother's duplex in the Union-Kinsman neighborhood of Cleveland, not as rough as Hough, the city's most depressed area, but rough enough. Just the other day, she says, Warren witnessed the robbery of the corner bakery. Before that he had wanted to be a baker. Now he wants to be a magician.

Moby had taught Phyllis to swim in 1980, but she had never thought about swimming as an activity for her children until she happened to see the Barracudas practicing one night at the college. "It was just amazing to see these kids swimming," she recalls, her face animated. "I had never seen children swim competitively. The fact that they were black and that they could swim that well fascinated me. I thought, Hey, those could be *my* kids down there."

Phyllis is the backbone of the Barracudas Swim Club, the team's support group. Even without a car, she tries to make every practice and every meet and has become quick with a stopwatch. It is an enormous sacrifice. "I've changed my life for this team," Phyllis says. "I've changed my schedule at work. I used to be able to go to concerts, to go partyin'. I could go out of town. On August first and second I wanted to go to New York for the weekend, but we had an intersquad meet. Tuesday I wanted to see Whitney Houston but we had practice. I say to myself, There'll always be another concert. There'll be a time for me."

Considering the alternatives available in the children's lives, Phyllis feels the sacrifices are worth it. "The kids have an uncle that used to be a heroin addict," she says. "He used to live with us. He's out of the house now, but we used to have terrible fights. I tell especially Warren, If you ever be like your uncle you won't stay with me.

"Quite a few of the parents, they don't have that father figure who is there," she says. "I know I don't, all right? Moby can talk

better with Warren than I can. A boy needs that. He's hit 'em
with kickboards, thumped 'em on the head, yelled at 'em, made
'em run and do push-ups. He'll cuss at 'em, but sometimes that's
the only thing that'll get their attention. It's not like they never
heard cussing before. Sure he's gonna be a little short-tempered.
He's lucky if he gets four hours of sleep a night. But Moby takes
an interest in the kids, which is very rare. It's not surface. It's
coming from his heart."

■

The Barracudas can afford to go to only a few meets each year,
usually after they've managed to raise money through a swima-
thon, where every lap swum generates a few cents from a pledger.
The meets are always out in Lakewood or Shaker Heights or in
some alien setting. The moment of truth comes when Moby, the
kids, and their mothers climb out of the van, brace themselves,
and walk together into one of those pool complexes. "You get the
looks," Phyllis Moore says, snapping her head to attention. "It's
like 'Oh my God I didn't know there was so many of them,' or
'I didn't know there were any black swimmers.' "

There are other tough moments as well. The Barracudas don't
win many races in the big meets, and, while their performance has
improved steadily since 1980, there are many races in which a
Barracuda has been the lone black swimmer, in last place, feeling
if not hearing the laughter, burning with humiliation, wanting to
be anywhere but there. Eleven-year-old freestyler Roberto Cottingham, when asked to state his goals as a swimmer, answers
casually that he would like to beat every white person in the world,
just to put an end to all the laughter.

Moby knows that debilitating feeling of freakishness, of novelty, the sense that every game for you is an away game, better
than any of them. A generation before, his own dreams of Olym-

pic fame and black history died in the Lakewood pool, a place
where the Barracudas sometimes swim. In the early sixties he had
been a precocious backstroker, at least by downtown standards, a
chunky boy who achieved a sense of identity and pride in being
able to defy both his body type and all the racial stereotypes.

And it hadn't been easy. He went into water over his head for
the first time on a dare and nearly drowned. He was taught the
four strokes by the camp counselor who rescued him—and whose
nose Moby broke in the process. Before long the Fairfax YMCA
pool became his habitat, technical journals his literature, Olympic
gold his dream. At a time Jim Brown was running over linemen
for the Cleveland Browns, Moby's hero was Johnny Weissmuller,
the first great Tarzan, and an Olympic swimming hero.

In 1963, Moby and his father carefully charted a five-year plan
that would put him in the 1968 games as America's first prominent black swimmer. The local trials were held at Lakewood in
June 1967. Moby entered the 100-meter freestyle and the 100-
meter backstroke. All he had to do was make the qualifying times,
times he had made in practice, and then it would be on to St.
Louis for the regionals and Portland, Oregon, for the Olympic
trials.

But as he warmed up on that hot day his feelings swung between invincibility—after all, he held thirteen city records and
almost never lost anymore—and the sinking feeling that he was
up against much faster competition that he had ever faced before.
He was king of Cleveland, he kept telling himself, trying not to
look around. He probably held more records than all of them
combined.

The gun sounded for the 100 freestyle and Moby got off fast.
As he approached the wall, he somersaulted and thrust his legs out
for a kick turn, a turn he had always hated to practice and rarely
needed to win his city meets. To his horror, he missed the wall

entirely. The judges disqualified him for failing to complete the course. Later that day he struggled, demoralized, through the backstroke event, completing it in a time too slow to advance. The memory remains raw twenty years later. "It's like the little fish in the small pond, who's the bully of everybody, but when he ends up going into the big ocean, he finds out he's a little fish, and there's big fish all around. There is a difference."

A generation later, the Lake Erie League pools still feel like oceans. And still there for Moby's young swimmers is the muscle-tying, mind-distracting intimidation that comes with having big fish all around. Phyllis Moore's ten-year-old son Warren describes what it feels like to climb up on the starting blocks, the only black swimmer at the moment of ultimate exposure, when a race is about to begin. "When I'm up on the blocks and I'm the only black person I feel terrible," he says. "If they all beat me I feel terrible. Moby tells me, 'Don't think about finishing last, just make your times.' But when you look around and you're the only black people there, you feel like everybody's givin' you the eyeball. Sometimes they say, 'What are *you* doin' here?' Sometimes it's like they don't wanna be in the same pool with us . . . I wish there were more of us."

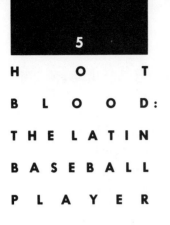

5

HOT
BLOOD:
THE LATIN
BASEBALL
PLAYER

Baseball is the only sport left of America's big three with a predominately white cast of players. The heritage, literature, iconography, and lore of the national pastime is that of white men in flannels, of Shoeless Joe, of the Babe, of Joltin' Joe, to whom our nation turns its lonely eyes. Of The Natural.

After a generation during which black participation increased steadily, professional baseball has been losing good black athletes to basketball and football for about fifteen years now, and college baseball is a decidedly white sport (a 1987 NCAA poll showed no black baseball coaches at 103 Division I colleges). "Baseball's not seen as the way out of the ghetto anymore," says Larry Whiteside, who covers the Red Sox for *The Boston Globe,* and who is black. "Other things are now. Baseball is the last of the avenues for kids to come out on now. Baseball has become a game of suburban leagues and superior coaching and all that stuff. It's only an option now."

But the Latin player is an altogether different story. In 1987 Latins outnumbered blacks in the major leagues, and over the last twenty years the percentage of Latin players in the major leagues has doubled to about 12 percent of the total. A growing number of today's stars are Hispanic, players like José Canseco, George Bell, Bobby Bonilla, Andres Galarraga, Tony Fernandez, Teddy Higuera, Fernando Valenzuela, Willie Hernández, Pedro Guerrero, Tony Peña, and Benito Santiago.

Latins have increased their numbers despite efforts to regulate their entry into baseball. In 1974 the U.S. Labor Department initiated a quota restricting the number of foreign-born players—almost all of whom are Latin—who can enter U.S. professional baseball to what has turned out to be between 5 and 10 percent of all players entering the minor leagues in a given year. The quota has operated without any serious opposition by major league baseball, and has managed to stem what would almost certainly be a riptide of Latin players.

Many Latins view the quota as a heavy-handed way to keep the national pastime's complexion white. "Whether it's the government, the commissioner's office, or whoever, people keep trying to keep the Latin kids out of the U.S.," California Angels manager Cookie Rojas told *The Boston Globe* in 1985. "They're crazy. . . . Do they think their fans are so prejudiced that they don't want to see Tony Fernandez or Pedro Guerrero or Joaquín Andújar or Willie Hernández or Tony Armas? You'd think the government would want these people as role models for the Latin kids in Los Angeles or the Bronx or Boston."

Indeed, as baseball seemingly strains to hold the line, the American population is becoming browner all the time. The number of Hispanics in the United States has increased 30 percent since

1980, to 19 million. Many of the new Americans have arrived from nations with rich homegrown baseball traditions. By the year 2000, if present trends continue, 15 percent of our people will be of Latin ancestry, and an estimated one third of the 30 million Hispanics will intermarry with non-Hispanics.

Though most fans don't know it, Latins have been in the big leagues for three quarters of a century now. There were Cubans, Puerto Ricans, and Venezuelans—carefully selected for their light skin—in the major leagues long before Jackie Robinson played. Likewise there were three American-born Hispanic managers— Mike Gonzalez, Al Lopez, and Preston Gomez—in the major leagues well before the first American black filled out a lineup card. Latins have produced a galaxy of stars with names like Clemente, Carew, Aparicio, Marichal, Perez, Tiant, Minoso, and Bell, most of them natives of Caribbean nations with baseball-rich traditions.

But despite their accomplishments, Latin baseball players have from the beginning been presented to U.S. fans in miniature, as moody firecrackers with short fuses, as snappy fielders with light bats, as homesick men who go away with the songbirds in the winter and sometimes come back in the spring. To white fans, the Latin baseball player is a cheerful, peppery character from south of the border, a stablemate of Cisco and Pancho, Cheech and Chong, Ricky Ricardo, José Jimenez, Trini Lopez, and Walt Disney's motor-mouthed, cigar-chomping parrot José Carioca. To U.S. fans, the Latin player is just happy to be here. *"Beisbol,"* says comedian Garrett Morris's Latin shortstop, "has been berry, berry good to me."

Latin players who lose their tempers are not flaky like Bill Lee or aggressive like that joyful throwback Pete Rose or scrappy like Billy Martin. The angry Latin is said simply to be crazy, plumb loco, the sorry victim of overheated blood. "The media creates images," second baseman Damaso García has said. "I'm supposed to be 'moody.' Sure I'm quiet, but all Latins are 'moody' or 'hot-tempered' or 'crazy,' right? Ask Mario Soto or [Joaquín] Andújar. They're supposed to be crazy, aren't they? When do you ever hear about Latins being leaders on a team?"

A decade after his retirement, Rico Carty, a Dominican native who was the major league batting champion in 1970, still remembers the sting of the notion that he, as a Latin, could not control himself. "When you cannot express yourself the way you want to, you get frustrated," Carty says. "Then everybody says, 'They're hot-headed, hot-blooded Latins.' But it's not that. Now that I can speak the language I can defend myself with words. But when you can't, all you have left is to fight to defend yourself."

Like many Latin players, Carty's frustration began early. He was first spotted as a seventeen-year-old, playing in a Pan-American game. After Carty showed an amazing arm and powerful bat, U.S. scouts fell on him, shoving contracts in his face. He signed thirteen of them. "My English was just not good enough," he recalls. "They were saying, 'Yes, you can sign, it's no big thing,' so I signed. I kept on signing. I signed with nine major league teams and four Dominican teams. I was lucky, because I didn't take any money."

After he got his legal problems disentangled, Carty signed for real with the Milwaukee Braves for a bonus of $2,000, a small fraction, he later learned, of what he would have received had he grown up in the States. He got on a plane, flew to Atlanta, and found his way to Waycross, Georgia. On the field, even though he couldn't understand much of what the coaches were saying, he nodded. He tried to ask questions, and to converse with his teammates, but the words rarely seemed to come out right. When he allowed his frustration to surface as anger, he began to hear that he was "hot-blooded." It took him years to develop a response.

"Finally, I decided just to smile all the time. Even if I strike out or make an error I smiled. 'Smiley with the white tooth,' they called me. That way I didn't get mad. Because if I got mad, I just couldn't perform."

Anyone who has spent time abroad knows that living in a new country is difficult. Japanese baseball teams try their best to ease the shock by providing live-in translators and paying whopping salaries to U.S. players who play in Japan. Still, very few American players last more than a year there. By contrast, American teams require Latin players to make wrenching and instantaneous transitions that would cause anyone's blood to boil. "I think most of these clubs are stupid the way they sign these kids, bring them over here and then let them rot on their own," Howie Haak, a Pittsburgh Pirate Caribbean scout, told *The Boston Globe.* "It's amazing how many have made it. The first thing is the food. They come over here and get sick. They want rice, beans, and chicken. Their systems have never had steak and milk, and they don't like it. Then there's the language. And if a kid can't pick up English in two summers, he's gone because the minor league managers start saying the kid's dumb. We've all heard that. . . . How well would a sixteen-year-old farm kid from Iowa do over there?"

The Latin baseball player arrives in America with a six-month visa, feeling, as Panama's Rod Carew once put it, "like a guest in someone else's house." Besides the requisite dietary, linguistic, and logistical adjustments, he finds himself caught out between black and white, a dark-skinned foreigner. In all likelihood, he has an intimate aquaintance with poverty, but having come from a land where races mix freely, little experience of racial prejudice. "Money counts in the Dominican—good job, what family you come from—not color," says Rico Carty. "In the States it's different." George Bell, the 1987 American League's Most Valuable Player and a native of the Dominican Republic, started in Helena,

Montana, in 1978. He found the experience jarring. "They [the fans] really dislike the black American guys," he told Toronto writers Phillippe Van Rjndt and Patrick Blednick in 1984. "It kinda hurt me a little bit because we don't see this here [in the Dominican Republic]. Everybody here lives with each other no matter what." Bell reported that Helena's white fans warmed up to the Latins once they overheard them speaking Spanish, a thaw that then created resentment from American blacks.

The Latins' in-between status in American baseball spills over into management too, where blacks and Latins feel themselves in competition for whatever minority slots may be available on a team's coaching staff or in its front office. Immediately after the Al Campanis flap, baseball teams produced lists of their "black" players and coaches for head-counting journalists. When Latins were included, thus increasing the total, some American blacks objected. "The Red Sox say they've got [coach] Felix Maldonado and [Rafael] Batista," complained George Scott, an American black who once played first base for the Red Sox. "Well, they're not blacks. Walk up to a guy like Pedro Guerrero and say he's black and he'll want to fight you. He doesn't want to be considered black. I'm a black American, that's what I am, and that's different. When you're talking black, you're talking George Scott and Frank Robinson."

The Latin has always been big-league baseball's cheap labor, its migrant worker, the boy who starts as an infant with a cardboard glove, reaches baseball maturity early, and would gladly play for free. According to Kevin Kerrane's study on scouting, *Dollar Sign on the Muscle,* "The average player selected in the June [1984] draft in the United States could expect to receive a bonus of $60,000. Latin American players with comparable tools were often signed, or purchased from a local team, for under $5,000."

Today, as yesterday, the Latin baseball player steps off a plane in Miami, holding on to a visa and a bus ticket or searching for a connecting flight, trying to read a menu, hoping to be met. He knows that tens of thousands of his countrymen would do almost anything to be in his shoes. Even though he has won his visa by beating out scores of other prospects, the odds are one in a hundred against him. Given the poverty of his homeland and the chance of a lifetime for wealth and glory, one thing is certain: He is indeed very, very happy to be here—even if only on a six-month visa—and determined to succeed.

■

From the time, probably in the 1870s, that American servicemen stationed in Cuba first introduced baseball to the Caribbean, the racial identity and specific color of the Latin baseball player has been of interest to major league baseball. Cubans loved the game immediately. By the 1880s, there were already hundreds of baseball teams throughout Cuba and several squads of Cuban players in the United States.

Word that there were accomplished players in Cuba, players whose skills were honed by year-round playing, reached American baseball owners quickly. But race—or more precisely, color—was a delicate issue. In the mid-1880s, two American blacks, Moses Fleetwood Walker and his younger brother Welday, had played for the Toledo Blue Stockings of the American Association—a precursor to the major leagues. But by the turn of the century, racial attitudes had hardened and clubs had taken a stand against signing Negro players. In Cuba, where there was no official segregation, you could find good ballplayers in all colors, but there was no way, owners assumed, that white fans would accept players who could be presumed to be Negroes. The trick, for major league owners interested in the Cuban players, was to find out exactly how dark a player could be and still be acceptable in the United States.

Thanks to John J. McGraw, at least everyone knew how dark
was too dark. In 1901 McGraw, as manager of the New York
Giants, tried to pass off a black bellhop named Charlie Grant
whom McGraw had seen stabbing grounders at an Arkansas hotel
as an American Indian named "Charlie Tokohama." Charles
Comiskey, owner of the White Sox, was the first to see through
McGraw's gambit and object. McGraw quietly backed down.

In 1911, Cincinnati Reds owner Garry Herrmann took a more
deliberate approach. He dispatched a team of Cincinnatians to
Cuba to find light Cubans and to obtain documentary evidence,
somehow, that their veins were free of Negro blood. The committee came back with two players, carrying certification provided by
Cubans that the two were "pure caucasian." They were outfielder
Armando Marsans, who played with the Reds, St. Louis Browns,
and Yankees until 1918, and third baseman Rafael Almeida, who
played with the Reds until 1913.

Black Americans took great interest in the two Cubans. Donn
Rogosin's book on Negro baseball titled *Invisible Men* contains
the following passages from a 1911 editorial in Booker T. Washington's *New York Age,* outlining a path for American ballplayers
with dark skin: "Now that the first shock is over it would not be
surprising to see a Cuban a few shades darker than Almeida and
Marsans breaking into the professional ranks. With the admission
of Cubans of a darker hue in the two big leagues it would then
be easy for colored players who are citizens of this country to get
into fast company . . . the Negro in this country has more varied
hues than even the Cubans . . . until the public gets used to seeing
native Negroes on big league [teams] the colored players could
keep their mouths shut and pass for Cubans."

So it was that until major league baseball was integrated, the
Latin player's prospects in the States depended entirely upon the
hue of his skin, the coarseness of his hair, and the look of his facial
features. If you were too dark, like Cuba's great Martin DiHigo,

who excelled at all nine positions and hit for power, you played in the Negro Leagues. If you were light, like pitcher Adolfo Luque, who was born about fifty miles from DiHigo, you could play in the majors. Some were in the middle. "Rough hair" kept the Giants from signing Cristobel Torrienti, a rugged outfielder. Light-skinned American blacks were counseled by scouts to go to Cuba, learn to speak Spanish, and come back as Cubans.

The most prominent preintegration Latin player ever was Luque, who pitched for, among others, Cincinnati and the New York Giants in the teens, twenties, and thirties. Luque was a small, serious Havanan with a sharp, knee-high curve that he could direct with great accuracy. His early success quickly caught the attention of a New York paper, which in 1913 assured its readers, "Luque is a very light skinned Cuban, in fact lighter than Marsans or Almeida, and looks more like an Italian than a full-blooded Cuban."

Luque, who today is all but unknown, won 197 major league games in a twenty-year career with four teams. He pitched in the majors until he was forty-five. He hit his stride in the 1923 season, when he simply tore up the National League. He won twenty-seven games for Cincinnati that season, the most in the major leagues, lost only eight, and led the major leagues in earned run average and shutouts and was second in strikeouts and winning percentage. Had there been a Cy Young Award, Luque would have won hands down.

Luque endured long after Marsans and Almeida, and was for several years referred to as "baseball's only alien." He was baited brutally and constantly; he once bloodied Casey Stengel's nose—the event for which he is best remembered by old-timers—after a tirade of abuse from the New York Giants bench that, as columnist Arthur Daley put it, persisted with "words that no descendent of the Spanish grandees could endure." But unlike

Jackie Robinson, who traveled a steeper but similar path years later, Luque, as a pitcher, held a weapon in his right hand. It was this advantage, and his willingness to use it if he had to, that gave him, and perhaps all Latin baseball players after him, the "hot-blooded" tag.

Almost everything ever written about Luque, even in eulogy, referred to his boiling blood, his love of cockfighting, his hilarious constructions of the English language—"I peetch outside curve. He sweeng"—and his alleged amorality when it came to throwing at batters. "When Luque got out on the mound, his blue eyes blazed malevolently at each hitter," wrote Daley in *The New York Times* after Luque's death in 1957. "He was a mean cuss at times and they said he never threw a beanball by accident. Whenever he hit a batter with a pitched ball, it was because he intended to do it."

"He would have been at a loss pitching in the big leagues today, when a pitcher must not hit a batter on purpose," agreed Frank Graham in his eulogy for the *New York Journal American*. "Whenever he hit a batter, he meant it."

"I don't think anyone tried to know him," recalls Jack Schwarz, Giants scouting director for nearly fifty years, who knew Luque as a Giants coach. "To say [his temper] was all there was to him—that's all the writers saw because it was interesting to the public. I never even really saw him as hot-tempered."

Toward the end of Luque's career, sportswriter Cullen Cain tracked him down in Cuba, and found a different man than he had expected. "He is earnest and serious," wrote Cain. "He is devoted to baseball heart and soul. . . . I wanted to know how a lad of an alien race had come to be such a whale of a pitcher. 'You just have to love baseball a lot,' he explained in halting but earnest fashion, 'and study it all the time and figure it out and give up a lot for it and keep trying and trying and trying.'"

∎

Latin players are often said to arrive, like produce, as part of a "crop" or "harvest." Their homelands are viewed as colonies, sites for makeshift scouting operations that deliver produce to the commonwealth of clubs up north. First one island or small republic will get hot, and scouts will wear out the soil, and then another place will catch fire, like the Dominican Republic today—until the competition becomes too ravenous, and the scouts will move on.

The first and all-time record-breaking bumper crop came from Cuba, courtesy of a laundryman named Joe Cambria. In the early 1930s, Cambria, a baseball fanatic who owned a neighborhood laundry in Baltimore, scraped together $5,000 and bought the Albany, New York, franchise of the International League. Cambria sold several of his players to Clark Griffith, the tight-fisted owner of the Washington Senators. It was a great deal for both: Griffith got players dirt cheap and conditionally—he paid Cambria only if a player made it to the Senators—and Cambria got to rub elbows with his heroes in the big leagues.

Before long Griffith made Cambria a scout, with no authority to spend money and on a strictly commission basis—he was paid if players worked out. That was fine with Cambria. He believed in signing players first—to stake them out—and then scouting them. If a guy worked out, fine; he would register the contract with the commissioner's office. If not, what the hell. Ballplayers waving their copies of Cambria's unfiled contracts poured into Commissioner Kenesaw Landis's office, but always Clark Griffith was able to save Cambria's neck.

Cambria made a living hustling the sandlots and amateur leagues of the Mid-Atlantic states until he happened upon Cuba. When he put two and two together, it seemed too good to be true:

▲ BYRON DAVIS, AMERICA'S FASTEST
HIGH SCHOOL FREESTYLE SPRINTER.

▲ THE 1924 U.S. OLYMPIC SWIM TEAM, FEATURING SEVERAL HAWAIIANS, WHO SURPRISED WHITE AMERICA BY BEING NOT JUST BUOYANT, BUT FAST.

▼ THE CLEVELAND BARRACUDAS, WITH THEIR COACH, CLARENCE "MOBY" MCLEOD.

▲ TRACY LEWIS, PRESIDENT OF THE
FIRST BLACK-OWNED BASEBALL
TEAM EVER AFFILIATED WITH THE
MAJOR LEAGUES, WITH A FAN IN
SAVANNAH.

WASHINGTON POST PHOTO BY LUCIAN PERKINS

▼ MIAMI KICKER REGGIE ROBY, THE ONLY BLACK KICKER OUT OF FIFTY-SIX IN THE LEAGUE AT THE END OF 1987, AND PROBABLY THE BEST KICKER IN THE NFL.

▲ MIAMI CENTER DWIGHT STEPHENSON, ONE OF TWO BLACK STARTING NFL CENTERS. BOTH STEPHENSON AND INDIANAPOLIS COLT CENTER RAY DONALDSON ARE PRO-BOWLERS.

◄ THE DODGERS' BASEBALL ACADEMY IN THE DOMINICAN REPUBLIC, HACKED OUT OF A SUGAR FIELD AND LOCATED ON AN UNMARKED ROAD, A PLACE THAT THOUSANDS OF KIDS FIND EACH YEAR.

▶ RALEIGH "BIZ" MACKEY, GREAT DEFENSIVE CATCHER OF NEGRO LEAGUE BASEBALL, MENTOR OF ROY CAMPANELLA AND EARL BATTEY.

▼ TOMMY LASORDA OUTWITS THE "HOT-TEMPERED." LATIN.

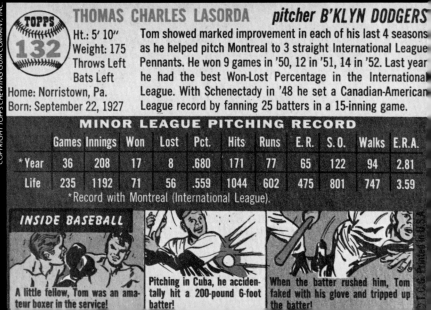

TOPPS 132

THOMAS CHARLES LASORDA   *pitcher B'KLYN DODGERS*

Ht.: 5' 10"
Weight: 175
Throws Left
Bats Left
Home: Norristown, Pa.
Born: September 22, 1927

Tom showed marked improvement in each of his last 4 seasons as he helped pitch Montreal to 3 straight International League Pennants. He won 9 games in '50, 12 in '51, 14 in '52. Last year he had the best Won-Lost Percentage in the International League. With Schenectady in '48 he set a Canadian-American League record by fanning 25 batters in a 15-inning game.

MINOR LEAGUE PITCHING RECORD

	Games	Innings	Won	Lost	Pct.	Hits	Runs	E.R.	S.O.	Walks	E.R.A.
*Year	36	208	17	8	.680	171	77	65	122	94	2.81
Life	235	1192	71	56	.559	1044	602	475	801	747	3.59

*Record with Montreal (International League).

INSIDE BASEBALL

A little fellow, Tom was an amateur boxer in the service!

Pitching in Cuba, he accidentally hit a 200-pound 6-foot batter!

When the batter rushed him, Tom faked with his glove and tripped up the batter!

▲ KIDS PLAYING BASEBALL WITH A HEWN BAT AND A ROLLED-UP SOCK, CONSUELO SUGAR FIELD, DOMINICAN REPUBLIC.

▼ FIVE YOUNG SHORTSTOPS AT THE TORONTO BLUE JAYS' BASEBALL ACADEMY IN THE DOMINICAN REPUBLIC.

The place was crawling with good ballplayers, some of them nearly white. They would play for almost nothing, were desperate to enter the big leagues, knew nothing about contracts, and he had the whole island to himself.

He set up shop in the Pan American Building in Havana, started dressing in a white linen suit and a Panama hat, and began scouting the sugar-mill teams, making arrangements with the owners. Before long he was signing Cubans by the carload for Griffith's inspection—over four hundred in one decade alone. Everybody knew Cambria, even though he never really bothered to learn Spanish. He would pretend to interpret for Griffith by shouting, in English, the questions Griffith put to him for translation. By sending Cuban players to the States, Cambria became a hero in Cuba. They even named a cigar named after him, "the Papa Joe." It beat starching collars in Baltimore.

Cambria's strongest bull market was during World War II, when the draft took most of the major league baseball players. The 1944 Washington Senators had a dozen draft-exempt Cubans in their spring-training camp. Latins were always hazed, but then it was at its worst. Not only were they not white and not American, but they were considered cowards as well; they were playing while Ted Williams was fighting. Bowing to public pressure, in mid-1944 the Selective Service ruled that Cubans living in the United States must register for the draft. Cambria's market nosedived.

After the 1947 integration of baseball, Cambria could at last go after Cubans of any hue. Until he was forced out of business in 1961 by Fidel Castro—a pitcher Cambria had twice rejected—Cambria's mother lode included some nuggets like Pedro Ramos, Camilo Pascual, and Zoilo Versalles. Versalles, the 1965 American League MVP as a shortstop for the Minnesota Twins, was a typical Cambria product. Intimidated by his second-grade teacher, Versalles quit school and never went back. He grew up playing baseball barefoot in the streets of Havana's Marianao district, a precocious boy always making teams stocked with men. At fifteen, his coach, one of Cambria's many bird dogs, sent Versalles and his mother to the Pan American Building in Havana. Versalles signed for carfare and later found himself on a plane to Key West, knowing no English, ordering food by pointing to photos of hamburgers, trying to figure out how to find the bus to his assignment in a place called Charlotte, North Carolina.

When integration opened the floodgates, and even the darkest Latins became fair game, scouts began to scour the Caribbean for prospects. An ex-catcher named Howie Haak took to roaming the tropics for Branch Rickey and signing the likes of Roberto Clemente, Manny Sanguillen, Julian Javier, Tony Armas, and, later, Tony Peña. Haak went places Cambria would never have ventured, by boat and plane and even mule into the jungle, places with no roads. He even stole some of Cambria's unsigned contracts.

Black and Latin players were, for the first decades after baseball's integration, wedged apart by the widely held, and widely denied, belief that they were competing against each other for a precious few positions reserved for minority players on each team. "Me, I'm a double nigger," Roberto Clemente once observed to writer Roger Kahn. "I'm a nigger because I'm black and a nigger because I'm Puerto Rican."

Most Latins learned in their homelands to field with one hand. But when they snapped down pop-ups and stabbed at grounders in the States without using a supporting hand they found, to their suprise, that they were committing in the opinion of American fans and coaches not technical errors but acts of outright blasphemy, flaunting a moral commandment—always use two hands—that American fathers had passed to their sons for many generations. Venezuela's Chico Carrasquel was probably the first infielder to use the one-handed technique in the States, but his countryman Luis Aparicio who, along with Cleveland first baseman Vic Power popularized one-handed fielding in the majors, caught the greatest hell for it.

As a young man Aparicio had inherited the local team's shortstop position from his legendary father in a solemn public ceremony. The aging father had handed his glove to the boy, given him a blessing and a tearful embrace, and walked away from the middle infield forever. As luck would have it, Aparicio's first manager in the States was Marty Marion, the exemplar and patron of the classic two-handed style. Marion was forever grumbling to writers in hotel lobbies about Aparicio's style. "He can dive for spectacular catches, but the glove dangles off his fingers," he told Chicago writer Dave Condon. "On the slow grounders I can't see how he can get solid contact with the ball. I'm going to ask him to use a glove small enough to feel a ball."

Many of the first postintegration Latin players were flown straight into minor league towns in the Jim Crow South, not knowing what to expect. Rico Carty remembers wandering into the white side of a segregated restaurant in Waycross, Georgia, in 1960 while his black teammates remained on the black side. "Everybody stopped eating and started staring at me. I was the only black person on that side. I couldn't speak English so I said in Spanish, 'I want to eat.' I got lucky. There was a family there who had just come back from the Dominican Republic. The man ordered my food. Everything came back to normal and people started eating again. When I was finished, I went back to where the other black players were eating. They said, 'Where you been?' I told them. They said, 'You crazy—they'll hang you over there.' I said, 'They hang me for eating?' "

In his autobiography, *The Way It Is,* Curt Flood wrote movingly of his own ambivalent feelings toward a Latin player, Cuban Leo Cardenas. Flood and Cardenas spent the summer of 1956 in Savannah, Georgia, as the only dark-skinned players on the Savannah squad. It bothered Flood that the team had found a home for Cardenas with a Spanish family, while he, Flood, felt alone and isolated in a strange southern town: "He [Cardenas] remained fairly happy all summer, drawing comfort from the many hours he spent with countrymen," Flood wrote. "Furthermore, they fed him. I was jealous."

And yet, Cardenas was black, and as such he was a countryman. Flood tried his best to interpret America for Cardenas: "His bafflement about the customs of the region was inexpressible. Time and again, when we were walking down the street of a Southern town, Leo would point to a comfortable-looking restaurant and say, 'We go there.' 'We can't,' I'd reply. 'Why?' 'They don't like us.' '*Like?*' 'They don't want us.' 'Why they no want us?' 'They don't want black people.' 'Why?' "

■ ■ ■

Pre-Castro Cuba remains the sweetest deal major league baseball has ever had, a baseball colony built on an island of sugar. The island was small, easy to scout, and Joe Cambria had built an elaborate scouting infrastructure, organized around 161 sugar mills of the island, each the center of a unique social organism called a *batey*. The typical sugar *batey* consisted of a general store, a police office, a narrow-gauge railroad network, the mill, a cluster of houses, maybe a school, and usually a modern, spacious, and well-lighted baseball stadium.

Almost every mill had a team, a team that provided first-rate equipment at local expense. The Cincinnati Reds, through an exclusive arrangement with the Havana Sugar Kings, made off with the likes of Tony Perez, Leo Cardenas, Cookie Rojas, and Mike Cuellar. Rafael Avila, Latin American scouting director for the Los Angeles Dodgers, remembers growing up in one of Cuba's sugar towns. "I come from a town named Ciego de Avila," he says. "We had nineteen sugar mills around us. Every one had a team. Tony Perez came from there, and Bobby Ortiz. The sugar mill was the center of everything."

Ever since Castro slammed the door shut in 1961, major league baseball teams have struggled to find something as good as Cuba. But it hasn't been easy. Puerto Rican baseball players, scouts complain, bound by the rules of the U.S. major league amateur draft, are too expensive and soft. Mexico for some reason seems to produce mainly pitchers. Venezuela is too mountainous to scout efficiently, Nicaragua too hazardous, and Haiti too French.

Today, no place on earth is producing more or better or cheaper players per hectare than the Dominican Republic. This tiny nation—it shares with Haiti an island whose land mass is a little smaller than Vermont and New Hampshire combined—was the birthplace of ten 1987 Toronto Blue Jays and eight 1988 Los Angeles Dodgers (counting players on each team's forty-man protected roster). The Dominican firmament includes stars like George Bell, Pedro Guerrero, Tony Peña, Tony Fernandez, and Joaquín Andújar. On one day, April 27, 1986, nine Dominican shortstops played major league games, seven from a single Caribbean port; if New York City were to produce players at the same rate, all twenty-six rosters would be filled with New Yorkers, and another 350 standbys would be waiting in the wings.

A visit to the Dominican Republic offers a look at the modern machinery of a form of exploitation that is at once racial—in that a totally white group of baseball executives is able to control the supply of and grossly underpay an almost entirely dark-skinned labor force—and partly a matter of habit, in that baseball had always regarded the Hispanic baseball player as, simultaneously, a migrant worker and a crop.

The Dominican offers baseball a tax-free business environment, exemption from the U.S. amateur-draft rules, a skilled work force trained at Dominican expense that will gladly start at any age and for a tenth the price of an American worker, and hundreds of villiage tipsters who will refer prospects to paid scouts for a very small commission. There is a superb infrastructure of stadiums and training facilities, built without cost to American baseball. The sugar mill—the most efficient machine ever known for manufacturing baseball players—still squeezes out Dominican players as it once produced Cubans. Best of all, there is the servile Dominican government, slavishly grateful for the reflected glory, which asks nothing of major league baseball.

It took many decades for major league baseball to prepare the Dominican soil for cultivation. The game was introduced to Dominicans by two Cuban brothers named Aloma in 1891, and a highly competitive league of mill teams around San Pedro de Macorís was operating as early as 1912. But for more than a quarter-century, at a time when light-skinned Cubans, Venezuelans, and Puerto Ricans played in the U.S. major leagues, the Dominican Republic was to major league scouts a mysterious and forbidden land.

Scouts were kept from observing the crop by Rafael Leonidas Trujillo, a brutal dictator who took over the nation in 1930. Trujillo had first observed baseball's hold on his countrymen as a policeman in the sugar fields near San Pedro. When he took over the country, in addition to renaming towns, rivers, and mountain ranges after himself, Trujillo set up a national baseball league, built four monumental stadiums, and took personal control of one of the teams, the Escojido Leones, based in the capital city (now called Santo Domingo but then known as Ciudad Trujillo).

Trujillo kept the Leones stocked with the Dominican's best players. He controlled their whereabouts and monitored their performance carefully. They were not to leave the country without his permission, and they were not to play for any other team but Escojido. There are still many Dominicans who can remember watching Escojido shortstop Andre Rodgers, having made a crucial error in a play-off game, stand frozen in position as Trujillo vaulted out of his box to strike him in the face.

While Trujillo's players were decidedly off-limits to U.S. teams, he once raided black players from the States to help solve a political crisis. In October 1937, not long before a rare national election, Dominican voters heard shocking reports that Trujillo's army had casually massacred over fifteen thousand Haitians in a weekend attempt to "clean up" their mountainous and indistinct border. In several areas, Trujillo's troops lined up and decapitated with machetes all those who pronounced with French intonations the word *perejil,* or parsley. When Dominicans reacted with an outpouring of grief and rage, Trujillo moved to shore up the Escojido Leones as a way to pacify voters in the capital city.

He dispatched a man named Frederico Nina to Pittsburgh with instructions to bring back the best Negro players he could get. Nina booked a room, spread out a suitcase full of currency on the bed, and invited the Pittsburgh Crawfords to behold the spectacle, one at a time. Nina came back with eighteen Negro League players, including Satchel Paige—whom Trujillo once jailed as a training precaution the night before he was to pitch a crucial game for the Leones. Trujillo's raid on the Crawfords put an end to one of the greatest Negro teams ever. For a while the players barnstormed the Caribbean in style as the "Trujillo All-Stars."

Even after the major leagues were integrated in 1947, bargain-hunting scouts, free to sign players of any complexion, avoided Trujillo's stronghold. But in 1955 the New York Giants hired Alex

Pompez, an ex–Harlem racketeer who had for years owned teams in the Negro baseball leagues, and who had scouted the Caribbean extensively. Pompez insisted the Dominican was crawling with great players and that he knew a way to pry them out. The Giants' brass, with little to lose, sent Pompez and a second scout named Frank "Chick" Genovese to Ciudad Trujillo to see what they could do.

Pompez, through his friend Horacio Martinez, an Escojido coach, somehow got Genovese hired as the manager of the Escojido team. That gave Genovese all winter to cultivate the Trujillo family, a job that kept him constantly on edge. The break came when Genovese gained the fast friendship of Trujillo's beloved son Ramfis, an impressionable young man who had been a full colonel in the army at age four and a brigadier general at nine.

At season's end, "El Benefactor," as Trujillo was called, dispatched his brother-in-law to New York to meet with Jack Schwarz, then director of the Giants' minor league operations. "We went out to lunch together," recalls Schwarz. "I only met the man once. Nothing was signed, no money was exchanged. It was just a handshake. The arrangement was, we would send a certain number of players down there for winter ball on the Escojido club, and we would have the first crack at any of their players. And they had all the best players."

In no time, the Giants were loaded with Dominicans like Felipe, Mateo, and Jesus Alou, Juan Marichal, Manny Mota, and Ozzie Virgil. The Giants' infiltration of the Dominican Republic remains a chestnut of scouting lore, a heist that broke new soil and set the stage for today's boom in Latin player development. "It was thanks to Alex Pompez that we even heard of the Dominican," recalls Schwarz, now retired, with evident satisfaction. "Pompez and Genovese made a great team. And Martinez was the local man. Really, he deserves credit for the wonderful harvest . . . it was just a great bit of scouting."

■

Six years after the Giants' breakthrough, Trujillo was gunned down on a moonlit road and the nation, after thirty-one years of his brutal rule, lapsed into a national coma. The winter leagues were canceled for two years and, except for a few diehards from the Astros, Pirates, and Dodgers, major league scouts vanished. Even the Giants, their arrangement terminated by Trujillo's death, disappeared.

But as salaries increased in the States, the need for cheap labor became acute. In 1961, the year of Trujillo's death, the average major league team spent $750,000 on player salaries. By 1980, the year Toronto Blue Jays scout Eppifino "Epy" Guerrero opened in the Dominican Republic the first full-time baseball "academy," average payroll had increased sevenfold. Beyond that, scouting had stagnated into a stale kind of espionage. In 1965 major league baseball instituted a draft system for amateur players in the United States and Puerto Rico designed to reduce the size of bonuses by eliminating competition for players. To old-line scouts, the draft all but ruined their profession. What good was it, they asked, to go to the trouble to find a kid if it meant having to hide him from the other clubs—which was impossible—dealing with their grasping agents and obnoxious fathers, competing with self-righteous college recruiters, and having to convince the front office that the kid was even worth drafting?

It is small wonder, that after a few years of dormancy, baseball rediscovered the Dominican Republic. It is a draft-exempt place that combines scouting convenience (a scout can traverse the nation's entire six hundred-kilometer border in a single day, holding impromptu tryouts all along the way), a joyous, homegrown baseball tradition, and the preeminent advantage of a good old-fashioned, soul-crushing poverty.

The Dominican has become to major league baseball what

Watts or Bedford-Stuyvesant is to college basketball: a place down so far that everything, especially something in the middle infield for, say, Los Angeles, looks like up. The average Dominican's gross annual income is now less than $1,000 and there is an official but underestimated unemployment rate of nearly a third. Cutbacks in the U.S. sugar quota in 1986 devastated the Dominican's major export industry, and the country's economy sags beneath a massive foreign debt. It has been estimated that in recent years, 150,000 Dominicans have risked their lives trying to cross a shark-infested channel to reach Puerto Rico or Miami. As the legendary Caribbean baseball scout Howie Haak has put it: "When was the best time for developing white players in this country? In the Depression. Well, in the Dominican and parts of some other countries, they're living in their own depression."

The Dominican Republic has become the new Cuba, a time warp, an out-of-the-way rendezvous for nostalgic baseball men, a fantasyland where kids "still want it" the way they used to in the States, even if most of them are too dark to have played in baseball's flannel days. Hunger is romanticized as a healthful incentive there. "I see kids playin' here like they used to in the States," says Phil Regan, a Dodgers pitching coach who coaches a winter-league team in the Dominican. "I actually saw kids bounce the ball against the wall and catch it with cardboard gloves. No wonder they have good hands. When they get a real glove it's nothing. They're hungry. It's their way off the island." The Dodgers' Rafael Avila agrees. "In the States and in Puerto Rico they got too many other things to do," he says. "They got a chance to work in the factory. They got a chance to go to college. In the Dominican they can't do anything else."

Baseball scouts find it easy to work with a client group that has no real options, away from the college recruiters, free of the disinterested blacks and spoiled whites of the United States. In this age of million-dollar salaries, the young Latin, a boy who has never met an agent or a college coach, is a sight for sore eyes. "Here, most of the kids you offer three or four or five thousand, they take it," says Julio "Sijo" Linares, Pan American scouting supervisor for the Houston Astros. "Nobody [the teams] has to pay any tax here and the players are cheaper and you can find a bunch of players nearly every day. They just keep coming. Maybe every month you will get one. Every player in Puerto Rico is asking for thirty or forty thousand dollars now, and I read in the paper where a guy from Puerto Rico got two hundred and twenty thousand. The most I ever paid was eight thousand. He run good, had good power."

Alfredo Griffin, the American League Rookie of the Year in 1979, signed with Cleveland for $2,500, against the advice of relatives. He was thrilled to do so. He had grown up in the sugar *batey* of Consuelo, where he had played with a rubber ball in the streets even as a small child. "My father-in-law said, 'That's not enough,' " Griffin recalls. "I said, 'It'll come in the future.' I don't know what I would have done if I hadn't signed."

Part of Latin America's special appeal to major league scouts lies in the chance for teams to avoid increasingly bitter—and successful—competition from U.S. college baseball. Professional baseball offers the prospect a career whose life expectancy is about two years and whose failure rate is around 99 percent. More and more kids who are able to choose between a couple of years of bus rides through the bushes and a chance for a diploma are enrolling rather than signing. "Kids are smarter than that now," says *The Boston Globe*'s Larry Whiteside. "Baseball might offer a good athlete a hundred thousand dollars. A good college might offer a four-year scholarship worth eighty thousand. If you're the mother, you might say, 'Hey, wait a minute. Maybe he should get the degree.' In baseball, the failure rate is incredible."

While the college-trained U.S. prospect is not ready to enter the minor leagues until he is in his early twenties, Dominican and other Latin players often sign at age sixteen. Before major league baseball adopted what is known in the industry as "the Jimmy Kelley Rule"—requiring players to be able to prove they have reached their sixteenth birthday or their junior year in high school at the time of signing—many started even younger. The rule is named after one of Toronto Blue Jays scout Epy Guerrero's signatories. "The reason that came about was not because Epy wanted to sign a thirteen-year-old boy," explains Gordon Ash, director of minor league operations for the Blue Jays. "It was because five other clubs wanted to. We liked him, but we wanted to do with him like he [Epy] did with Tony Fernandez—'You work out with me, you play, and then, when you're old enough, we'll sign you.' But it got to the point where too many other clubs were trying to sign him so we had to. Everyone would say, 'You bad guys, signing a thirteen-year-old player.' We'd rather not have, but the bottom line for Epy is to sign quality players, and Jimmy Kelley was a quality player. He's on our forty-man roster now."

The stampede to sign Dominican bargains has created a classic scouting pyramid, where a successful referral can bring a tipster precisely calibrated commissions that last through a player's career. Houston's Julio Linares, a Dominican native who spent fourteen years in the Giants and Braves chains without ever coming to bat in the majors, does his best to explain how it works. "Well," he says, "right now Houston got four scouts here. They make six or seven thousand dollars if they work in a small area, maybe twelve if you cover a lot of ground, that's U.S.A. dollars, plus expenses. That is a living wage here. Then there have got to be over a hundred bird dogs.

"A bird dog has a contract with the player. If he brings me a

player I might give him [the bird dog] a hundred dollars. If the
players makes Double A, the bird dog gets five hundred dollars
and a thousand for Triple A. If I'm not mistaken he gets two
thousand five hundred U.S.A. dollars if he plays for the Astros."

But, says Linares, holding up his hand, that's not all. "You see,
the problem is between the bird dog and the guy who just comes
in and recommends a player. The guy who just brings a player in
here—this is a guy who is not a bird dog. We sign the player and
the guy says it is not enough, so I give him five hundred. . . . You
know, this phone rings all the time. It's unbelievable. Most of the
time the guy can't play but you've got to go see because you never
know. Sometimes you would like to be with your family maybe on
a Sunday and there is a ball game somewhere and you have to go.
It is a very tough job."

■

The baseball "academy" is the institution of higher learning that
is responsible for the great Dominican harvest of today, and which
has ushered in what might be called the "agrobusiness era" of
Latin American player development. The baseball school gives
teams a chance to put a few hundred dollars down on a kid and
board him for up to three years until they decide whether he is
worth a visa to the States. "Here in the Dominican you can sign
'em for five hundred or a thousand and just put 'em in the
academy," explains the Dodgers' Phil Regan. "You're supposed to
wait till they're sixteen, but . . . You know, everybody criticizes
these academies but, hey, it's just like school: Ya get the kid off
the street, give 'em three square meals a day. They love it."

Epy Guerrero, who built the first academy, is acknowledged by
all to be the Dominican's master scout. Guerrero was rescued
from his father's grocery store by current Toronto general manager Pat Gillick, then just starting out in the Houston front office

in 1967 when the island was still in its post-Trujillo hush. Gillick hired Guerrero part-time and asked him to develop local talent. In no time, Guerrero had produced, through local tryout camps, one Cesar Cedeño, who became the star of the Houston team. "After that Pat said, 'Forget about the store, you're a scout now,' " laughs Guerrero.

Guerrero stuck with Gillick as he jumped from Houston to the Yankees and finally to Toronto, producing a steady stream of major leaguers, which today includes Toronto stars George Bell and Tony Fernandez, all for sub-$5,000 bonuses. In 1980, Guerrero asked Gillick for money to build a training center where he could teach and observe the players he signed. He wanted a place of his own, free from government restrictions, out of the way. He knew a guy with a gambling debt who would give him land in a sugar field just north of Santo Domingo for $50 a month. Gillick said yes.

Today, eighteen teams and counting have followed suit, crowding their schools like suckling pigs around the sugar mills of San Pedro de Macorís. The teams have even established, through collective funding, a sixty-two-game winter league, a kind of countercultural substitute for the official and infinitely more expensive minor leagues of the United States.

It would be all but impossible to find the Toronto Blue Jays' academy without a guide. Like most of the others, it is located on an unmarked road, hacked from an ocean of head-high green stalks of sugarcane. The school consists of a small dormitory, kitchen, classroom, and office. Outside, there is a small diamond with a viewing area, another small field in a terrace below, two batting cages, and two pitching mounds. Barbed wire surrounds everything but gaps in the fence. On a November afternoon, a cow patrols the right-field line. "You'll notice that the *complejo* is out in the middle of nowhere," says the Jays' Gordon Ash to a visitor. "We did it on purpose. We wanted a degree of privacy. But everybody has the wrong impression. These are not concetration camps for future players."

The Dodgers' "Campo Las Palmas" is, by contrast, a sort of baseball Club Med, replete with stables and orchards, first-class weight rooms and training facilities, two full diamonds, the Walter O'Malley Headquarters Building, and, of course, the Tommy Lasorda Dormitory. The Dodgers would prefer you not ask how much the academy cost. "It wasn't as much as people think," says Rafael Avila, who runs the complex. "People think it cost a million dollars. It wasn't even near that."

Each morning by seven Avila finds six or eight or ten boys lined up along the first baseline. Some have gloves. Each is waiting for his chance to run sixty yards for a coach, make a few throws, and take some swings in the cage. The odds of success are roughly that of winning a state lottery, but Avila estimates that the Dodgers turned away two to three thousand walk-ons last year. "The good thing is so many come," sighs Avila, gazing out over a balcony at the catch of a winter midweek day. "But that's the bad thing too. Do you realize what an enormous sacrifice they make to come out of these little sugar towns and be here at seven o'clock? They know where we are. Sometimes I can see the disappointment in their eyes.

"One day," says Avila, "I guess the grass was too high at the sugar mill or something, but sixty pitchers came to try out. By six-thirty in the afternoon I had only seen eighteen of them. I wanted to go. But my scout said, 'No, we gotta see one more kid.' He throw his first pitch. *Boom!* "I said, 'Gimme that [radar] gun.' He throw again. *Boom!* Eighty-six. His name was Valdino. We just traded him to Detroit. That's the thing. You gotta see them all."

The Dominican baseball student has little time for academic

learning. "Yesterday, if someone wanted to be a professional, they played in the street and didn't have to worry too much," says Atlanta Braves shortstop Rafael Ramirez, who grew up near the Angelina sugar mill in the preacademy days. "But now the people ask you for more. They have a baseball school now, and you have to make up your mind what you are going to do, if you want baseball, or to go to school. They start you out early in the morning, and when they are there they work really hard. You get out late. If you want to go to regular school, you go at night."

No Juilliard violin prodigy works any longer or harder than a Dominican baseball student. "We go fifty-one weeks a year, six days a week," says Avila. "There is a week off for Christmas." And they are long days, filled with classroom instruction, films, calisthenics, and baseball games. The Dominican baseball student leaves the academy with a world-class education in ground balls and a few words of technical English. The luckiest of the vast majority who fail are able to find work with a mill or factory that has a team, or get to play for the military police.

"We're really teachin' 'em," says Avila. "When we send 'em to the U.S. we can be sure they play baseball the way it should be played. They get a good baseball education, plus we bring in an English teacher an hour a day, a girl from Santo Domingo. We give all the instructions in English. When they say, 'I got it,' we say, 'Take it.' Maybe they don't know what it means, but they know they're supposed to say, 'Take it.' "

■

Asked why he located the Dodgers' academy near one of the San Pedro mills, Rafael Avila offers a simple explanation. "If you're gonna build a factory that makes shoes," he explains, "you're gonna put it where you can find leather." Like Joe Cambria, who formed his Coffee-Colored Brigade from the sugar mills of Cuba, the Dodgers and the other teams who cluster their academies around the seven mills of San Pedro know the sugar mill as a machine that squeezes out tropical baseball players.

Entering the 1987 baseball season, thirteen residents of greater metropolitan San Pedro de Macorís—including the eighty thousand residents of the town proper and the fifty thousand others the *bateys* organized around seven nearby sugar mills—were on major league rosters. George Bell, Joaquín Andújar, Julio Franco, Alfredo Griffin, Pedro Guerrero, Mariano Duncan, and many others grew up in mill towns, where family members built, ran, dusted, and repaired machinery, sold candy in the streets, and loaded carts with cut cane.

Today, some of them have become millionaires, especially in pesos. Three miles by railroad from the poverty of the Consuelo *batey* is a stucco enclave of Dodgers and Jays and Astros, a world of satellite dishes and attended gates that swing shut, often with young girls hanging on them, behind pastel-colored touring automobiles. Alfredo Griffin's next-door neighbor on one side is pitcher Joaquín Andújar. Braves' shortstop Rafael Ramirez is breaking ground on the right. George Bell is building across the street. Rico Carty, the Dominican's first big hero, lives a couple of blocks away.

Juan Castro, as director of sports for the Consuelo Sugar Company, the largest of San Pedro's seven mills, built the teams on which several big leaguers were first scouted. The walls of his small office outside the mill are papered with fight photos and covers of American sports magazines. Mickey Mantle beams from these walls. The young Ali stands cursing over Floyd Patterson. "The goal of all boys here is to be signed [by American baseball]," Castro explains. "They can even be seen by scouts in our minor league. Of course, the Consuelo team is a big goal too. If they make it, they have a better chance to get a job in the factory."

It is an ancient incentive, a job at the factory, not all that different from that offered to the father of the East German gymnast or the father of an exceptionally tall high school kid in Indiana. "The native, his major worry is to have employment," says Castro. "There is no security until you have worked twenty-five years with the factory. Then we give you a pension at seventy-five percent of salary." Since no factory worker at Consuelo makes a daily wage that could buy breakfast in downtown San Pedro, or a monthly wage that could secure a night's room at one of the nearby resorts, it isn't surprising that Consuelo's boys would prefer a chance to wear a Blue Jays uniform to a chance to clean the rollers that squeeze nine tons of cane into a ton of sugar.

But even as major league teams are planting their baseball schools around the mills, investing for a long-term harvest, the mills themselves are dying. Sugar, the product that once was a pleasant lump in every American's morning coffee, is now regarded by many as "white death," something that can be made from beets and corn and chemicals by American workers. The Angelina mill, the old haunt of Braves' shortstop Rafael Ramirez, shut down in 1986. Juan Castro worries about the future of Consuelo. "The price is now twelve cents per pound," sighs Castro. "Three years ago it was twenty-seven cents. We just fired about twelve percent of the workers. The U.S. is just hanging us with these prices and quotas."

In such an atmosphere, Castro says he has begun to feel squeezed himself by the U.S. teams who cluster their academies around the mills and cruise the sugar teams for prospects. "The work that I do is free," he says. "I earn a salary here because I work in the sugar factory. We create the baseball players. My thought is baseball's investment should be bigger. We need roads. We don't have a center of entertainment for the kids. There are no bathrooms at the school." Watching the sun crawl across the great barrel of the Consuelo refinery, Castro says he has his own economic proposal for the United States. "Maybe if sugar prices were based on the number of baseball players produced," he says, "we would be winning."

Castro is not alone in wondering whether the United States could do more. Along with feelings of pride and reverence for the local heroes of San Pedro de Macorís, hailed as the baseball capital of the world, there is a growing resentment in the Dominican Republic by players, local scouts, and community leaders, especially around San Pedro, a feeling that their players are yet another cheap U.S. crop, something to be consumed out of the country and regulated by quotas.

The players themselves, many of whom frankly admit that they would have signed for nothing for a chance, often react angrily when they get to the States and find out what their often less-accomplished U.S. counterparts are earning. "You always have the feeling you gonna have a tough time getting what you're worth," says Houston's Linares. "When they sign and go to the States they hear that some guy got forty and they got three, they walk around with the feeling they're gonna get released. I have to tell them, Don't worry about that."

Many Dominicans are coming to feel that baseball should reinvest some of the take created by the exciting Dominican players in the nation itself. There have been minor investments, especially by Toronto, and by some of the players who return in the winter, who involve themselves in civic projects. But some would like to see baseball teams help build real schools as well baseball academies. "Baseball causes a good effect," says San Pedro de Macorís teacher and historian Miguel Piri, "because they give the city a good name. But they should do more. They should make some schools and day-care centers or libraries. The money they pay those players could give benefits to the town. They should do it because they have gotten a lot of benefits."

"If these top scouts would call the owners and say, 'Well, Mr.

O'Malley,' or 'Well, Mr. Steinbrenner, we need a school here,' they would do things for this country," says Rico Carty. "But nobody will ask them. They're too busy telling the owners they can get Dominican players for less money than the American scouts can. So why should [the owners] do it? Maybe O'Malley knows the needs of the Dominican people, but someone has to ask him, and the scouts are afraid."

Most infuriating of all to many Latins is the quota on foreign-born baseball players entering the United States that has, for the last decade and a half, had the effect of limiting the alien baseball population to between 5 and 10 percent of all players entering the minor leagues in a given year. It is the Dominican ballplayer, perhaps the world's most thoroughly scouted athlete, a boy fattened on dreams of becoming the next George Bell, signed for a few hundred dollars and educated in ground balls and baseball English, who feels the quota most profoundly. The odds against making the majors are tough enough anyway, they say—why establish competition for a visa as yet another filter? "Why can't baseball really be an international sport?" Epy Guerrero has demanded. "Why does it always have to be controlled out of New York?"

Major league baseball's attitude toward the quota has been divided along the lines of each team's involvement in the Latin market. Latin marketeers rail against the quota, while teams who rely on homegrown talent insist that our boys must be protected, like Fords and Chevies, from the cheap immigrant tide. Every now and then the commissioner's office goes through the gesture of asking each team how many visas they need, adding up the total, and preparing statistical support for a request to the Labor Department for exactly that many visas. In 1987 the number was 530.

It is hard to say whether organized baseball inspired the quotas, but it is clear that the commissioner's office hasn't resisted it. "When you have three to four million kids in the U.S. playing baseball," says George Pfister of the commissioner's office, "the U.S. Labor Department says, 'Why do you need foreign players?' We have to prove to them that we've exhausted everything possible to find U.S. players, and that we're looking for *prospects*, top-quality players, and not just giving away jobs. It's good the way it is down there now. We don't want a lot of adverse publicity messing it up."

While many Latins, as dark-skinned people, feel the quota to be a product of racial prejudice, the Labor Department says that the quota exists solely to shield the U.S. player from the glare of competition. "We want to have a control on the number of foreign players who are being used," explains Michael Dougherty, a manpower development specialist who has administered the quota for the U.S. Labor Department for the past several years. "If [teams] can get Latin players cheaper on the sign-up bonuses, that would be an incentive for them to bring in many more, right? Well, what about domestic players? These are American employers. There are available American players out there. So why not have a control?"

It doesn't trouble Dougherty that American teams spend millions to cultivate the foreign competition from which we must protect U.S. players. What if, Dougherty is asked, the day comes that the Latin-market teams can show statistically that thousands of Latin players, trained monastically in U.S. baseball academies, and having grown up totally immersed in baseball as our children used to be, are better qualified for the major leagues than their suburbanized American counterparts? Would the door then swing open to greet them?

Dougherty takes his time. "I think, and this is just my opinion," he says carefully, "that there would be a big revulsion of the

American fan. We have a great baseball tradition in this country that the average American fan believes in. We still, I think, have the preponderance of talent out there. There are stars out there. There are. There's still a George Brett, isn't there? There's still somebody like The Natural out there."

Earl Battey was fourteen when he first noticed the stocky man watching him play baseball at the park near his grandmother's house in Los Angeles. It was 1949, a time when black boys throughout America wanted to be second basemen, just like Jackie Robinson. Not Earl Battey. He was a catcher, like his mother. For years he had watched her anchor a smart professional softball team, counseling pitchers and gunning down runners. For him there was no place like home.

He loved the excitement of being in on every single play, the chance the position gave to show off his powerful arm. Though he was only a freshman, Battey was already the first-string catcher for his high school team, and on weekends he caught for the Watts Giants, an adult men's team whose second baseman was his uncle Clifford. On summer days he would often visit his grandmother. There was always a game in the park, and there the man would be, leaning on the fence or sitting in the bleachers, often chatting with two or three others, but always watching.

When Biz Mackey finally introduced himself, it was their handshake that left a permanent impression on Battey. "It was like shaking hands with someone who had polio," he recalls. "A lot of catchers are that way. If a catcher was pointing out directions to you, if he was pointing straight the finger would make like a left-hand turn. I remember that about him."

On that day, Biz Mackey was an out-of-work catcher, drawn back to the old workplace like any early retiree. A year before he had been the manager of the Newark Eagles of the Negro National League, a championship team whose roster included Don Newcombe, Larry Doby, and Monte Irvin. But after Jackie Robinson had broken in with the Dodgers, those stars had been snapped up like peanuts by the major league clubs, the Eagles were sold, and Negro baseball was all but finished.

Biz Mackey had been widely regarded as the greatest defensive catcher in the history of Negro baseball. Even Com Posey, who had owned and managed the Homestead Greys when the great Josh Gibson was his star catcher, had told a reporter that Mackey's overall value to a team was greater than Gibson's. But now, that and a nickel would get him a cup of coffee. On the day Biz Mackey met Earl Battey, he was fifty-two, too old to catch in the majors, and it would still be a quarter-century before a black man would manage in the major leagues.

Earl Battey knew none of this. All he knew was that the big man knew more about the catching trade than anyone he had ever met. Their conversations began to take the form of an extended tutorial, a college in the dust that lasted throughout Battey's high school days. The first lessons were about different ways to set up behind the plate, and then about Battey's favorite subject, throwing.

Mackey could see that Battey loved to try to pick runners off base, but that he didn't really know how. It wasn't enough just to have a strong arm, Mackey told him. You had to pick your spots. There was a way, he said, to lull the runner on first base to sleep. You had to wait for a right-handed batter, so that your throw would be unobstructed, and throw on a pitch breaking away toward your right, so that your momentum would be going in the direction of the throw. As many American League base runners were later to discover, it worked.

Most of all, Mackey knew about pitchers. He had all sorts of practical tips for dealing with them. You had to be a communicator, he kept saying. Some you had to baby, some you had to rag constantly. There was a way to all of them; it was up to you to find it. It was fine to become a pitcher's friend, he said, but it was essential to command his respect. Battey remembers one ace that he pulled out again and again throughout his thirteen-year American League career: "Mackey said, 'If you don't think the pitcher is giving you one hundred percent, you just take two steps out in front of the plate and throw it back to him as hard as you can. Don't throw it at his glove. Throw it right at his testicles. He may miss it once but he won't miss it twice. That way you can rest assured you have his attention.'"

■

Unlike the black quarterback, who has rarely been given a chance in the National Football League, the black catcher has lost a position that he once occupied in numbers, and at which he once excelled. In the 1950s and 1960s, black catchers, including Battey, Roy Campanella, Elston Howard, John Roseboro, and Elrod Hendricks (who was born in the Virgin Islands), won four Most Valuable Player awards, seven Gold Gloves for defensive excellence (Campanella would surely have won more had his career not preceded the award), and played on many All-Star teams. But since John Roseboro hung up his shin guards in 1970, there have been only two black American starting catchers in major league baseball—Earl Williams, who caught for Baltimore, Oakland, and Atlanta in the early 1970s, and Cleveland's Gary Alexander, who last caught in 1980.

While there have never been many black pitchers in the major leagues, there has always been at least one fireballing standout—like Don Newcombe, Joe Black, Bob Gibson, J. R. Richard, Ferguson Jenkins, and Vida Blue. Today, black kids can look to Dwight Gooden, Dave Stewart, and Lee Smith as examples of powerful pitchers. But a recruiter of black catchers, should one ever arise, would face the same problem as, say, a recruiter of black forest rangers: You'd have to explain the job.

■

The first black baseball player to play professionally with whites was a fine defensive catcher named Moses Fleetwood Walker. Walker was the son of a Steubenville, Ohio, physician, born in slavery, who had traveled north to Ohio on the underground railroad. In 1884, more than a half-century before Jackie Robinson, Moses Walker played forty-two games for the Toledo Blue Stockings of the American Association. In addition, Moses's younger brother Welday, also a catcher until Moses's skill behind the plate put him in the outfield, played five games for Toledo that year.

The Walkers were cut short by one Adrian "Cap" Anson, a great hitter who was inducted into baseball's Hall of Fame in 1939. Anson had both an enormous influence on baseball in the 1880s and an obsessive hatred of blacks. When Anson's Chicago team traveled to Toledo to play the Blue Stockings, Anson refused to take the field until the Walkers were banished. Within a week they were out of baseball entirely. Moses Walker expressed his feelings in a letter of protest to the governor of Ohio. "The rule that prohibits colored men from competing in so honorable a pastime as baseball," Walker wrote, "is a disgrace to the present age and casts derision on the law of the land which clearly states that all men are created equal."

The Negro Leagues, which flowered from 1920 until the integration of major league baseball, gave birth to the first generation of major league catchers, men who had grown up admiring the great slugger Josh Gibson and a spate of defensive geniuses that included Mackey, Frank Duncan of the Kansas City Monarchs, and Larry Brown of the Memphis Red Sox. Each Negro League team had carried two or three catchers, some of whom had caught hundreds of games and handled top-flight pitchers by the time they reached major league baseball.

Roy Campanella, like Earl Battey, grew up with Biz Mackey as a tutor. In 1937, as manager of the Baltimore Elite Giants, Mackey heard about a chubby boy prodigy from Philadelphia who could hit like a man and had already caught for another Negro League team. After watching Campanella play, Mackey began to court the fifteen-year-old boy's parents, asking if young Roy could play just on weekends, then on summer vacations from high school, and finally as a tradesman.

Mackey ordered Campy to sit beside him on the bench and listen and learn to be a defensive catcher. Campanella recalled his education, flank to flank with Mackey in the dugout, in his autobiography *It's Good to Be Alive:* " 'There's so much to learn about catching, kid,' he'd say. 'There isn't a game in which you can't learn something, if you look for it . . . there ain't a player who ain't got a weak spot.' " As for pitchers, he told young Campy, "[a catcher] can make a fair pitcher look good by calling the right pitches. Or he can ruin him by calling for the wrong ones. You gotta learn to handle pitchers like they were babies sometimes, each one different. You gotta scold some, you gotta flatter some, you gotta bribe some, you gotta think for some, and you gotta mother them all!"

Catcher was the ideal entry position for eager black players when major league baseball was first integrated. Then, as now, there was less competition for the drudgery behind the plate than anywhere else on the diamond. "I tried catcher because I would have been cut loose from the ball club if I didn't catch," says Sam Hairston, who had spent his best years as a backstop for the Birmingham Black Barons before integrating the Chicago White Sox in 1951. "There wasn't another position open. They were gettin' ready to release me when the catcher got his finger broke. I had been a third baseman and a first baseman. I decided I could catch."

By the time Campanella first strapped on the tools for the Brooklyn Dodgers in 1948, beginning a ten-year career in the major leagues during which he won three National League Most Valuable Player awards, he was only twenty-seven, but already a twelve-year veteran, an accomplished catcher who had begun as an apprentice to a great master. By the time he hit the majors, he had squatted more times, soothed more pitchers, accepted more collisions, and spotted more weaknesses in batters than almost any of his contemporaries in the National League.

It took guts and maturity to be a black backstop in a white league in 1948, to tell white pitchers what to do while white batters waved a split of ash inches from your mask and white umpires steadied themselves with a hand on your back. Others might have found the experience unsettling, but not Campanella. Unsettling had been the day, long ago, when Mackey split his finger and second-string catcher Nish Williams got hurt too, and Mackey had told him to go in for the first time. Unsettling had been trying to learn on the job to catch baseballs covered with the mixture of slippery elm and chewing tobacco that was legal and fashionable in the Negro National League. Next to those days, the National League was nothing, no matter what people thought about your skin.

The first major league black catchers were countrymen bound together not only by the experience of estrangement as blacks in a white world, but also by split fingers and angled handshakes, creaky knees, and a catcher's distinctive sense of martyrdom. They knew, taught, and supported each other. "Back then there was no novelty about being a black catcher," recalls Battey. "There was Campanella, and me, and Valmy Thomas and Charlie White and Sam Hairston and lots of others."

Battey remembers staying with Roy Campanella in a segregated hotel in Tampa in the spring of 1954. He asked Campanella for advice on catching, an inquiry that quickly became a crash course. It didn't matter that Battey was nineteen and struggling to make the White Sox, while Campanella was the reigning MVP of the National League. They were kinsmen. "Campanella really prepared me for what was to come [in the major leagues]," recalls Battey. "He said, 'If you're truly interested in becoming a catcher, you have to know the psychological makeup of your pitcher.' He told me pitching is eighty or ninety percent of the game, and catchers are eighty or ninety percent of a pitcher. You're dealing with twelve different personalities, and you have to find a way to extract something out of each pitcher to make him give you what he has. He taught me that the way you do this is to get into all kinds of so-called unnecessary conversations with them, just to find out where their head is at."

The first generation was there to break in a bumper crop of successors, such fine defensive catchers as Elston Howard of the Yankees, John Roseboro of the Dodgers, and Elrod Hendricks of the Orioles. Late in his career, Campanella was assigned by the Dodgers to prepare Roseboro as a successor. Much of the training was off the field. "He befriended me and became like a father to me," Roseboro wrote in his autobiography, *Glory Days with the Dodgers and Other Days with Others.* "He became my roommate and guided me through the big cities—Philadelphia, Pittsburgh, St. Louis, Cincinnati, Chicago, and Milwaukee—as I traveled the big-time tour for the first time. . . . He taught me how to dress and took me to the finest stores and helped me shop for the right clothes. . . . He made me feel like a big leaguer."

"My biggest help was Valmy Thomas, who was also a black catcher," Elrod Hendricks recalls. "We played together on the Santurce ball club in Puerto Rico. I watched him. I watched how he handled himself and listened to him on the bench talking to pitchers. We talked only occasionally. He was from the old school and he didn't care to share a whole lot with me. But what he did share was cherished like gold."

■

Catchers are sometimes called (usually by catchers) the quarterbacks of a baseball team. Quarterbacks are rarely called the catchers of a football team. To a kid, a quarterback looks like a hero and a catcher looks like something from a natural-history museum. Quarterbacks get to stand erect and shout while everyone else bends over. On a baseball team, everyone stands but the catcher. The quarterback is clearly the protagonist of the offense. Catchers, by contrast, are said to "anchor" the defense. After a career of a hundred thousand squats, catchers end up looking like linemen, not quarterbacks.

"I can't get anyone to catch," complains Rafael Avila, director of Latin American scouting for the Dodgers. "Sometimes I think the problem is the parents. They keep saying they don't want the kids to get hurt. And I keep telling them with all the gear and everything, it's safer than the other positions. They don't believe it."

Nor should they. Retired catchers end up not only with crooked limbs, but with thickened frames bearing the dents and scratches that come from operating in heavy traffic. While outfielders preen themselves between pitches, catchers squat in the dirt beneath the batter, flashing furtive recommendations that pitchers feel quite free to scorn in full public view. Deep inside about fifteen pounds of modern chain mail, catchers have to worry about the pitcher's confidence, stuff, and alertness, the count, all base runners, impending collisions, the positioning of the other defensive players, the umpire's shifting stike zone and moods, each hitter's strengths and weaknesses, and how far it is to each dugout's top step. Despite all this, fans are most likely to notice a catcher when someone on the other team steals a base.

And there are hygienic problems down there. The Dodgers' John Roseboro wrote of catching beneath Frank Robinson. "He'd step in and spit, and if the wind wasn't right it would come right back through my mask. You hate to tell a guy to stop spitting and I didn't know if it was deliberate so I didn't want to start a fight for nothing."

Combine the position's troglodytic image and the absence of contemporary Campanellas or Josh Gibsons, and it's easy to see why young black kids aren't thronging to the shin guards. In fact, it's hard not to wonder why *anyone* would do it.

It seems to be a question only a catcher can answer. "I still preach to anyone of any race that catcher is a great position for starting in baseball," says Elrod Hendricks. "But catcher is not a glamorous position. The only reward you get is from within. It's the feeling of knowing that you have helped a pitcher. You also know when you haven't. We're a very small union. Not too many people want to get into it."

The answer seems to be that some few, once they put on the

tools, simply cannot imagine playing anywhere else. They come to view anything else as a part-time job. They love having the entire field in front of them and having so much to do with a game's outcome, even if nobody knows it. An outfielder gets to react maybe five times a game. A catcher initiates and handles maybe two hundred pitches. As ex–Cardinal and Philly backstop Tim McCarver put it, "I became a catcher because that's where the ball game is."

■

In the late sixties and early seventies, after the original reservoir of talent from the Negro Leagues dried up and their accomplished offspring retired, scouts and coaches began to put blacks behind the plate for a different set of reasons. They caught not if they could lead, analyze hitters, and communicate with pitchers, but by a form of default: They caught if they were (a) wide, (b) slow, and/or (c) unsuccessful at all other positions.

Since John Roseboro last caught for Washington in 1970, black catchers have been, for the most part, converted first basemen or outfielders, such as Atlanta's Rico Carty ("I hated the foul tips") or Cliff Johnson of the Astros and Yankees, or aging sluggers hanging on. The last two American black starters were Earl Williams of the Braves and Orioles in the mid-1970s ("He hated it with a passion," recalls teammate Hendricks) and Gary Alexander, an unpolished uppercutter who caught ninety-one games for Cleveland in 1979 and managed to lead the American League in errors.

Black baseball players have increasingly found themselves in the outfield, away from the positions where play is initiated and controlled. If you were a black baseball player in 1960, you were 5.6 times as likely to be an outfielder as a pitcher. By 1970, the ratio was up to 6.7, and 8.8 in 1980. Entering the 1987 season, almost two thirds of all black players were outfielders and 82 percent of all black offensive players were either outfielders or first basemen. In the 1988 All-Star game, promoted as a look at baseball's future since thirty of the game's fifty-six players were All-Stars for the first time, all twenty-four pitchers and catchers were white except for Dwight Gooden. Six out of the eight starting infielders were white. All eleven outfielders were black or Latin except for Boston's Mike Greenwell and Pittsburgh's Andy Van Slyke.

Being asked, increasingly, to chase after the ball a few times a game while others stand closer to the plate and make things happen may account in part for the steady decline of blacks entering baseball in favor of basketball and football (and, in part, for the absence of black managers, since managers are typically former catchers, middle infielders, and pitchers). The decline was first noticed, with some alarm, in the early seventies. While the teams remained mostly white, some of the game's greatest stars and most exciting players were black. To lose the supply entirely would be to threaten the gate. As *Sporting News* publisher C. C. Johnson Spink put it in a 1974 editorial, "We believe the decrease in the number of black players is a far more important problem than whether or not there is a black manager soon."

It can hardly be said that blacks have caught, pitched, or played the infield without distinction in their first forty or so years in major league baseball. Having played only a third as long as whites in the major leagues, blacks, according to statistician Bill James, have produced, at the peaks of their careers, history's greatest catcher (Roy Campanella), third greatest first baseman (Willie McCovey), two greatest second basemen (Joe Morgan and Jackie Robinson), and second greatest shortstop (Ernie Banks). And Ozzie Smith is now widely regarded as the best-fielding shortstop in baseball history.

Likewise, black pitchers have been among the statistical leaders at their position ever since baseball was integrated. Using 1986 team statistics, the Center for the Study of Sport in Society found that, by percentage, nearly four times as many black pitchers as whites had earned run averages below 3.00, and twice as many whites as blacks had ERAs above 4.00.

Some regard the stockpiling of blacks in the outfield and their scarcity on the mound, behind the plate, or in key infield positions as a sign that the whites who control baseball don't trust blacks to make decisions or initiate play. "You have to deal with the stereotypical attitude of the intelligence or capability of a black person to maintain a position like catcher," says Earl Battey. "The subtle message is that we have genetic talent, but we're just not intelligent," Reggie Jackson has said. "Aren't blacks smart enough to be starting pitchers or run games as catchers?"

But others, like Elrod Hendricks, now the Baltimore Orioles' bullpen coach, wonder if scouts, obsessed with the image of blacks as runners, even notice a black player's mind anymore. "For a long time, I guess the thinking was that blacks couldn't think," he says. "That they weren't smart enough to remember the hitters." Those days, Hendricks thinks, may be behind us. "They're lookin' for legs," he says. "They're sayin', 'Go get it! Run that ball down!' That's all they're thinkin' about, the legs."

Indeed, today's granite-hard synthetic playing surfaces have produced big-league careers for fast men who can learn to drive a pitched ball straight down without hitting their feet. One pioneer didn't even have to do that. In 1973, Charlie Finley, then owner of the Oakland A's, took it to the limit by hiring a black world-class sprinter named Herb Washington to do nothing but pinch-run. In 109 games, Washington never faced a pitcher or took the field. After his two-year career concluded, compilers of the *Baseball Encyclopedia* were stymied when it came time to identify Washington's fielding position. The guy had been a dashman. Finally they just left it blank.

Elrod Hendricks lays out the scout's view of a black baseball player, one that seems to start from the neck down. "If the guy can run, they'll put him in the outfield. If he has good hands and can't hit, they'll put him at shortstop. If he can swing the bat a little and has some power, then naturally they'll put him at first base. Now, if he's *extremely* slow, they'll put him behind the plate."

"It's a well-known thing that most of your black players can run and hit," said Cincinnati manager Pete Rose in a 1987 magazine interview. "Why ruin your speed being a catcher?" To Rose's question, experienced catchers might reply, "Why waste your mind in the outfield?" Catchers say that catching isn't about speed. It's where the ball game is. Catchers, talking about catching, sound like daytime talk-show hosts. They talk about how moody and sensitive pitchers can get. They use words like "giving" and "communication." "Just to go back there, to catch the ball and throw it and hit it, isn't enough," Roy Campanella has said, adding, "you have to be a communicator first." "Pitcher and catcher are one body," says Hendricks, his voice charged with the conviction of this irreducible truth. "You got to be an amateur psychologist."

It takes patience and a serious investment of time for a baseball organization to develop an accomplished defensive catcher. "More than any position, catcher requires an apprenticeship," says Earl Battey. "You won't see championship teams with rookie catchers. I don't think I would have developed the way I did if I had just come up after a short time in the minors, without a chance to play every day."

Patience may lie at the heart of the matter. Today's players reach the major leagues far faster than they used to, and arrive with less experience. "I wouldn't say that the average major league player was better in the old days," says Elmer Gray, the Pittsburgh Pirates' director of scouting, "but I would say that today's rookie is not what he was. You don't have the minor league veteran anymore. You got fewer minor league clubs [nine thousand minor league players in 1949 had dropped to thirty-three hundred in 1982] and more big-league slots. You gotta bring 'em along faster. The day of the ten-year minor league veteran is over."

Elrod Hendricks's Baltimore Orioles staff has become the closest thing in the majors to an equal-opportunity bullpen. The Orioles in 1987 had two of the four black catchers to appear on major league rosters. None of the four started, but the Orioles' Floyd Rayford—a converted third baseman since released—and Carl Nichols both saw some playing time. In Hendricks they have a professor who in 1971 caught one of history's great pitching staffs, when Jim Palmer, Mike Cuellar, Dave McNally, and Pat Dobson each won more than twenty games.

Hendricks has especially high hopes for the twenty-five-year-old Nichols. "He's gonna be a good one down the road. He's very sharp behind the plate, but he doesn't assert himself the way he should as yet. He just has to take charge a little bit more. He has a strong arm, he's a good receiver, he blocks the ball well, and he's a little bit different—he can run."

Hendricks says that prospects are brighter for Latin catchers—future Tony Peñas, Benito Santiagos and Bo Diazes—than for blacks, because the Latin leagues produce catchers, just as the Negro Leagues once did. "See, there's so many shortstops and outfielders down there that somebody has to catch," Hendricks explains. "In the U.S., as soon as a [black] guy can run a little they'll put him in the outfield, no matter what position he's played before because I guess the thinkin' is 'blacks can run.' If you'll notice, most Latins aren't very big. Those that are big and strong, they'll either put 'em in the outfield or behind the plate. There just aren't any [young black catchers] to draft. You see it in high school. Even in little leagues, they put black kids out at shortstop if they're tiny and in the outfield if they can run."

■

Earl Battey is today the same age Biz Mackey was when Battey first felt Mackey's eyes upon him at the park near his grandmother's house long ago. Their relationship probably meant as much to Mackey as it did to Battey; even if his livelihood was gone, life wasn't all that bad if there was still a young catcher good enough to get down in the dirt with and teach.

But times have changed in strange ways. Battey knows that as a black man, his chances of becoming a major league catcher, of having his leadership skills recognized and cultivated, were better thirty years ago than they would be today. "Right now, what role models do you have for a young black kid to become a catcher?" Battey asks. "There are none, so no kids go out for the position."

Temporarily, at least, blacks no longer occupy baseball's traffic-control center. Gone are the few sacred inches close to home where squats the only player who can behold the whole field of play—albeit through the bars of a mask. Throughout baseball history, great catchers, black and white, have been strong, tough, and shrewd, distinctive mainly for their ability to lead and communicate, not for the presence or absence of foot speed.

Catching hasn't changed. It is still the most demanding, least glamorous, most avoided, and most important place on the field: the ideal entry position. Long ago, an ex-catcher named Muddy Ruel dubbed the catcher's leaden gear "the Tools of Ignorance." The name stuck. But despite the position's pedestrian setting and medieval raiment, there is nothing ignorant about a good catcher. True ignorance resides with those who, in the blind quest for yet another pair of legs, would squander the leadership potential of black baseball players.

BASKETBALL:

TWELVE

THOUSAND

TO ONE

Paul Cook, assistant basketball coach at the University of Maine, has trouble attracting black high school seniors up to the spruce country of central Maine. "The University of Maine has ten thousand four hundred students," Cook says, "and thirty-nine of them are black. Twenty-six are on athletic scholarships and five to ten more receive athletic aid. . . . It's so different from the city. There's no black environment, no social life for them. It'd be like you or me going to Grambling."

But then Cook, like college coaches throughout the land, accepts it as an article of faith that his team can't win without black players. "We have to know about every available black kid out there that we have a possibility of getting, because it's tough for us up here," he says. As one college recruiter puts it, "Look, I don't want to be quoted on this, but what's the difference between a white player and a black player? If you set the ball out ten feet away and told 'em both to go after it the quicker kid'll get the ball. Same if you set the ball on the rim. Intelligence and determination comes into play, but all things being equal, the quicker kid'll get there first. And black is quick."

Black teenagers have become the hard currency of college basketball, the foundation of multi-million-dollar programs. Many if not most of America's top basketball players are young black men who count as assets a mother, several siblings, and with the jobless rate for black youth at 55 percent—about twice as high as that for whites—considerable time on their hands to play basketball. They learn to play a rough, compressed game, with, for boys, a form of manhood at stake.

Most major college programs hire at least one black assistant coach to venture into the places where tall, tough boys and girls— many of whom would be ignored, feared, arrested, or written off if someone hadn't noticed they could jump three feet off the ground—can be found. Many of them are found in playgrounds around schools that the Carnegie Foundation report on urban schools described in 1988 as "little more than human storehouses to keep young people off the streets."

In basketball, amateur or professional, one or two good players can mean a fortune. In 1986, Indiana University coach Bobby Knight grudgingly recruited two junior-college players, both black ("we *had* to get some athletes," his assistant coach Joby Wright told writer Bruce Newman, "players who could jump and were quick enough to play the game as it was evolving with the shot clock"), and turned the decision into a national championship and a huge payday. Advertisers paid CBS over a half a million dollars for each of twenty-eight minutes of advertising time in the 1987 NCAA final game. Indiana University, by winning the tournament, collected slightly over $3 million.

Given the stakes, coaches have become sourdoughs, feverishly pouring in and out of inner-city summer tournaments and summer camps, grubstakers who pack in tapes and clipboards, prospecting for nuggets, hungry for the fortune that lies in a propulsive pair of legs.

But no coach can see every prospect, especially since the NCAA allows only a few weeks each year for direct recruiting. When he needs more names or second opinions, Paul Cook, like coaches throughout the United States, turns to Rick Ball, a Missouri-based architect who publishes a junior-college scouting report called *Ballplayers,* to Tom Conchawski, who rates high school upperclassmen in his *High School Basketball Illustrated,* to Joe Butler's *Metro Index,* or to one of a dozen or so other publishers of scouting reports. Their thumbnail sketches, dashed off in the jargon of the trade ("superior IQ on the floor"; "great kid, great family"; "predictably slow and earthbound"; "associates the word 'jump' with a game of checkers"; "a miniature Charles Barkley"), read like real estate ads in the Sunday classifieds.

Along with appraisals of each player's height, leaping ability, grades, and toughness, most of the scouts are careful to identify each player's race in their reports with the initial "B" or "W" or the words "black" or "white." "Obviously," explains Cook, "if I'm looking for a black small forward, I don't want a white one. The big thing there is athletic ability."

"When I write up a kid, I try to describe them," says Tom Conchawski. "There are certain racial stereotypes like, a black kid is supposed to be more athletic and a white kid is supposed to be more cerebral. I use it because it's part of a description. When I write up a kid I put down 'B' for black, 'W' for white, and 'PR' for Puerto Rican. I don't think there's anything racial in it.

"Now, some schools need white players. Because they play a lot of black kids, because of the part of the country they're in, or because of their alumni or boosters, they've gotta have some white faces. Schools like, say, Vermont or Maine or New Hampshire—they don't have a lotta black kids. They know that they eventually want to attract better athletes, they want to attract black kids. So even though they might not be able to get an outstanding black player, they might take a lesser black player."

"Coaches want to know," says Bill Cronauer, a Saint Petersburg–based journalist who, with his partner Bill Bolton, prepares the *B/C Report,* another scouting report for coaches. "Trying to provide what college coaches want is our business. Remember, you got the real world out there. Without naming a specific school, I'm not saying they gotta have a white in the lineup, but, I'll tell ya what," he adds, laughing, "it sure doesn't hurt."

"I personally can't do it [list a player's race]," says Rick Ball. "But if a coach calls and asks, I'll tell him. [A coach will] say, 'I gotta have two [whites] for the team picture.' That's not unrealistic. It's still that way in business. Almost every major football staff has one black assistant. Not any more than one. Just one. I'll have a coach call at a school in the South and say, 'I need four players and one of 'em oughta be white.' "

Scouts have been providing racial information to college basketball recruiters since the sixties, when the nation's collegiate athletic conferences were being integrated. "I can tell you its origin firsthand," says CBS basketball analyst Billy Packer. "I went through this. The first scouting service was Howard Garfinkle's *High School Basketball Illustrated.* Howie got that started in the early sixties. In those days his primary subscribers were southeastern schools. During those days I was a recruiter. I was honest with those kids. Twenty years ago, black guys could not play in [certain] leagues. That's not just teams, that's *leagues.* I knew there was no way a southern team would accept a majority of black starters. I purposely would not recruit a player, knowing that he would be put in a position where he deserved to play because he was black.

So the scouting services were for coaches who said, 'Gee, I can't have more than this and I can't have more than that.' "

It is impossible to know how many players have been denied or given spots on the basis of the racial information contained in the reports. The players, who rarely see the reports, and who have no idea why they do or don't win scholarships, are in no serious position to challenge a selection. But that doesn't make the practice legal. "State schools are prohibited by the Fourteenth Amendment from discriminating based upon race or color," says Drew Days, a professor of law at Yale and formerly the assistant U.S. Attorney General for Civil Rights. "And even private schools, if they receive federal funds, are prohibited from accepting or rejecting athletes for reasons that go beyond their abilities and have to do with race. These practices raise serious constitutional and statutory questions as to their legality."

"I think that [publication of a player's race in scouting services] is disgraceful," says Packer. "I have never heard in recent years a coach say, 'Well, Billy, have you seen so-and-so play—well, is he black or white?' I can't comprehend why the 'B' or 'W' is on there today."

Joe Butler can, though, because he's in the market. Butler has published the *Metro Index,* rating players mainly in major eastern cities, for eleven years. He is asked why it is necessary to indicate a player's race on his scouting sheets. "Are you gonna publish this?" he inquires. He is told yes. "I do that," he begins, "because a lot of schools have financial-aid packages. They may have a black-studies program and they may be a predominately black university. They need to know the races . . ."

Butler stops, then starts over. "I don't understand why they do it," he says. "They wanna know. You oughta talk to a college coach. Call Indiana. It's such a touchy situation. I don't even know who would want to talk about it.

"I'd prefer not to do it. I list it because college coaches request this information. I don't want people breathin' down my back. I've had this business eleven years." He pauses again. "Just do me one thing, OK? If you print it, be sure to say I do it because the coaches want it, OK?"

■

Basketball is the first team sport in which white players can be seen as tokens. Fewer than forty years after the first black NBA player laced up his sneakers, nearly four of every five NBA players are black and black statistical domination of the league is nearly total. At the 1988 All-Star break, seventeen of the league's top eighteen scorers were black, as were eight of the nine top rebounders and nineteen of the twenty top assist makers.

The trend exists in college and high school basketball as well. Only a dozen years after then-Governor George Wallace stood in the doorway to block a black student from enrolling at the University of Alabama, the basketball team's five starting players were black. A few years ago in Cleveland a court-appointed officer, charged with implementing a plan to desegregate Cleveland's public schools, ordered that each of the city's fourteen public schools carry two *whites* on the basketball team. At the time of the order, there was only one white player in the entire Cleveland school system.

After years of unwritten quotas regulating the number of black players that would be allowed on each team, NBA teams now reserve the sturdier end of the bench for two or three white players in order to satisfy ticket holders who, executives apparently believe, would not pay to see an all-black team.

And while it is hard to understand how anyone could believe some of the Goliaths who fill out NBA rosters could sell tickets (in 1987 six of the only seven players who scored *less* than two points per game were whites who averaged over seven feet in height and 250 pounds), the gate value of a white player is no laughing matter. Using home-attendance figures for all games played by the twenty-three NBA teams in the six seasons between 1980–81 and 1985–86, University of Illinois professors Larry Kahn and Peter Sherer found, in a study published in the 1988 *Journal of Labor Economics* that "replacing a [black] player with a [statistically] identical white player could raise home attendance by 8,000 to 13,000 fans per season. . . . The lure of white players at the gate did not seem to depend on what proportion of the residents of the area were black." "What the data shows," says Sherer, "is that it makes business sense to, in effect, discriminate. The owners are giving fans the product they want."

The value of a great white player is almost beyond measure. According to CBS television statistician Linda Levins, after a decade of thrilling games, the NCAA championship game with the biggest television audience in history remains the 1979 match between Indiana State, featuring white star Larry Bird, and Michigan State, featuring black star Magic Johnson. Entering the 1988 season, games between Bird's Boston Celtics and Johnson's L.A. Lakers have captured most of the highest television ratings in the NBA's history. And one look at the 1989 draft list makes one wonder where the next Larry Bird is coming from.

The amazing thing is that the tide has turned so quickly. Until World War II, basketball was a game of white immigrant neighborhoods and farm towns. Few blacks really knew how to play the game until postwar basketball programs appeared in black community centers, and strips of asphalt were poured outside the huge housing projects in which so many northern blacks found themselves.

Despite the greatness of the New York Rens, an all-black squad that had easily dominated the best white professional teams throughout the thirties, the only black basketball players many of the early black NBA stars knew about were the Harlem Globetrotters. "The first I ever knew about basketball was the Globetrotters," recalls Oscar Robertson, who grew up in Indianapolis in the forties and fifties. "Goose Tatum and guys like that. I didn't know anyone else until later on, when the Indianapolis Olympians got a team. They are the only ones I remember seeing play."

The Globetrotters began as a dead-serious Chicago-based team that, in the late twenties, thirties, and early forties had been the equal of any of the white squads in the precursor leagues of the NBA. But in the forties their owner, Abe Saperstein, perceiving the possibility of a wider audience, turned the team into world favorites by pandering to white stereotypes of blacks as sly, loose-limbed, undisciplined clowns, in writer David Wolf's phrase, "Stepin Fetchit with a jock strap."

The NBA barred blacks until 1951, in no small part because Saperstein insisted on his right to monopolize black talent. It was a demand he was able to enforce by threatening not to make the hugely lucrative Globetrotters available for NBA pregame shows at a time when the league was struggling to stand on its own.

In 1951 the NBA defied Saperstein and drafted its first three black players, Duquesne's Chuck Cooper, West Virginia State's Earl Lloyd, and Nat "Sweetwater" Clifton, whom the Knicks got directly from the Globetrotters. It was shocking. Lloyd's parents were attacked in a crowd at one game. Richard Lapchick, son of Joe Lapchik, who coached the Knicks during Clifton's first year, has written of his experience as a small boy overhearing his father answer the telephone and realizing that they were death threats.

The outright color bar became an informally maintained numerical quota that receded, rather rapidly, position by position, until today many NBA teams have eight or nine blacks per squad. In his 1958 autobiography *Go Up for Glory,* Bill Russell wrote of the days when the number was three: "In this same year [1958], we [the Boston Celtics] acquired a fourth Negro player, our number-one draft choice, Ben Swain of Texas State. A sportswriter finally summed up what I had been talking about when he wrote: 'The Celtics will not keep four Negroes. The crowds won't stand for it, and neither will the owners . . . ' I seized on it. I brought the article to [owner Walter] Brown and [coach Red] Auerbach and said: 'Now, tell me.' "

Swain was signed, and seven years later the Celtics became the first team to play five blacks at once. "I didn't even notice it because we had practiced together," recalls Tom "Satch" Sanders, one of the five. "But Heinsohn was such a smoker, you know, and we needed a shooter. Naulls was it. I didn't think anything of it until Russell mentioned it after the game."

The following year the Philadelphia Warriors won the NBA title with a black starting five and and all-white bench, and, in 1979–80, the Detroit Pistons fielded what its ex-coach Dick Vitale believes to be the league's first all-black squad. "I didn't have three or four white tokens just to keep a season ticket holder," Vitale recalls. "I'm not that kinda guy."

Julius Erving is widely credited with rescuing the NBA from an economic slump and a sort of spiritual malaise in the mid-to-late seventies, in the dead years between thrilling New York Knicks teams of the early seventies and the Bird-Magic era of the eighties. Dr. J. saved the day by making the league, and the world, safe for dunking.

The dunk has long been a black cultural statement, a cause for rejoicing. For a period during the pitched racial tension of the late sixties and early seventies, starchy NCAA officials banned the dunk altogether. "The rule [taking the dunk away] wasn't put in to stop seven-footers," Robert Bowens—at the time a black assistant coach at Hunter College—told author James Michener. "It was put in to stop the six-foot-two brothers who could dazzle the crowd and embarrass much bigger white kids by dunking. . . . Everyone knows that dunking is a trademark of great playground black athletes. And so they took it away. It's as simple as that."

Erving brought a sense of artistry and style to dunking the ball. Somehow, he dunked with a cool combustion, an elegance that at once triggered black pride and excited—but did not threaten—white fans; it was more like watching a gymnast than a badass. Erving's off-court bearing was pleasant and civil, not militant. As the years went by he clipped his Afro and cultivated a corporate image. He was the ideal package for the NBA—at once a black man who dunked like no other and a safe hero for white kids.

The control position, the ball handler, which now gets called the "point guard," was the last position integrated. No black became an assist leader in the NBA until Guy Rodgers finished second in the 1959–60 season, long after blacks had become statistical leaders in scoring and rebounding. At the time the ball belonged to white crowd-pleasers like Bob Cousy, Larry Costello, Dick McGuire, Richie Guerin and Carl Braun, Bob Davies and Slater Martin. It might have stayed that way a lot longer had not Oscar Robertson, big, strong, and omniscient, so clearly in command that no one could challenge or deny his leadership, taken over the assist column and held on to it for the next decade.

Throughout college and high school basketball, the ball handler is the position most often filled by whites. In his book *Broken Promises,* written in 1984, Richard Lapchick found that while slightly more than two thirds of all college players were black, white point guards outnumbered blacks three to one. Georgetown basketball coach John Thompson explained how it happens to *Sports Illustrated* writer Bil Gilbert. "In basketball it's been a self-fulfilling prophecy," he said. "White men run the game. A white coach recruits a good black player. He knows the kid's got talent, but he also knows—or thinks he knows—that because he's black he's undisciplined. So he doesn't try to give him any discipline. He puts him in the free-lance, one-on-one hot-dog role, and turns to the little white guard for discipline."

While the NBA looks anxiously down the road for the next Larry Bird, some blacks view the prospect of an all-black NBA with a different kind of concern. For black kids, television offers no more potent image than the black basketball player, soaring over rooted whites, succeeding totally and with style. "It gets so that you think 'sports,' you think 'black,' " says Ed Jones of the National Black Media Coalition. "The television images reinforce the notion that a successful black male in America is an athlete in the NBA or NFL. That becomes the definition of success. Before that it was entertainment, and before that it was a preacher. The chances of a young black becoming Michael Jordan are off the scale. That's the damage."

For others, sports is yet another narcotic, a beautiful distraction that, in the absence of alternatives, becomes a life-sapping obsession. "Why can't the same planes and helicopters that bring football players and basketball players to our colleges come back with some potential doctors and lawyers?" Jesse Jackson has asked.

Sociologist Harry Edwards takes it to the limit. He believes the spectacle of so many blacks in sports trivializes blacks by allowing whites to keep on believing that blacks are engineered expressly to play games. "When sport becomes little more than a form of black cultural exhibitionism," Edwards told *Life* magazine's John Underwood, "white America—and you have to understand that nothing moves in this society until white sentiment makes it happen—white America will come to see sport in the same vein as it sees the Harlem Globetrotters."

■

If on the day Sam Drummer of Muncie, Indiana, first saw Kareem Abdul-Jabbar on television, Abdul-Jabbar could have hopped into

the Drummer living room for a counseling session, he could have at least offered some perspective. "Yes, I was just like the rest of those black athletes you read about," Abdul-Jabbar told writer Jack Olsen in 1968, the year Drummer first noticed him, "the ones that put all their waking energies into learning the moves. That might be a sad commentary on America in general, but that's the way it's going to be until black people can flow without prejudice into any occupation they can master. For now it's still pretty much music and sports for us."

But Abdul-Jabbar stayed in the set and Sam Drummer, amazed by what he saw, was changed forever by Abdul-Jabbar's style. "There was something about him, the way he could be so big and handle the ball. I remember settin' a goal after that. I set my mind that I was gonna work hard. I was gonna be a pro ballplayer. I guess that was in seventh grade."

Sam grew up in a housing project with his mother, Elizabeth, his brother, and two sisters. His father had left the household when Sam was three, and the family's principal income came from Elizabeth Drummer's disability check. "I was the oldest son," Sam Drummer says, "the man of the house. I wanted to take care of my family. I wanted my mom to have stuff. We never had nothin'. I was gonna turn everything around with basketball."

There was always a game at the housing project, and little else to do. At first the older kids laughed at him, but because he was tall and he could jump well from the start, they chose him. He improved rapidly. In eighth grade, a man named Roger Banks, who said he was a coach at a junior college in Boiling Springs, North Carolina, came around and told Sam he was going to be good someday.

Sam went to Muncie North High School in basketball-crazed Indiana, and made the basketball team in his freshman year. At that point, as a black high school player, according to a study conducted by Richard Lapchick, Sam Drummer's chances of making the NBA were about one in twelve thousand. Sam Drummer, like most of the others, felt destined to be the one.

In high school, he had the feeling that nothing was expected of him academically, just as long as he played. That was fair enough with him. Still, after Sam carried Muncie North to the finals of the Indiana state tournament in his senior year, he received well over a hundred invitations from America's institutions of higher learning. For a few weeks, Muncie's cloverleaf inns were jammed with college recruiters. "Here come all these people from all over the United States, offerin' money, cars, everything else," Sam recalls. "To be honest, I couldn't handle it."

He decided to follow Roger Banks, who had maintained contact with Sam throughout his high school career. "I depended on him," says Sam. "He was the only one I knew. He had started recruiting me in eighth grade. He got a job at Austin Peay, in Nashville, so I went with him. Then he got a job at Georgia Tech, so I went to junior college for a year, and got Junior College Player of the Year, and then I went to Georgia Tech."

As a black college player, Sam Drummer improved his chances of making the NBA—still his only goal—to 1 in 183. At Georgia Tech, Drummer majored in "industrial arts." "Mostly coaching courses and stuff," he recalls. "We read some blueprints. They were just to help me get through so I could play ball. It was, 'Here, you want a car? Take the car.' I'd say, 'I want this,' and they'd say, 'Yeah.' That made me think, 'Hey, I'm gonna make it. What am I worried about? All I gotta do is play ball.' I was drivin' a Lincoln Continental in college."

When Sam Drummer's four-year basketball eligibility expired in 1979, he had amassed about two years' worth of academic credits in largely worthless courses. But it didn't matter; the charade was over at last. He was free to ply his trade. Right on schedule, the NBA's Houston Rockets drafted him in the fifth round and invited him to rookie camp. With his destiny at last in sight, he celebrated in Muncie with his friends until they saw him off to Houston. The odds against him had shrunk to seven to one.

It wasn't until the third day of camp that Sam Drummer glimpsed the wall for the first time. "There must have been about fifteen or twenty rookies," he recalls. Mostly they were looking for guards. I had never played guard. I was six-five. I don't think they kept but one or two."

He remembers the flight back home to Muncie after he had been cut as if it had happened yesterday. "It was bad, oh it was bad," he says, laughing softly. "I was really hurtin' 'cause I knew all my friends were gonna be lookin' at me. All my friends, all the people around—they always knew I was gonna be playing pro ball. My mom and sisters met me at the airport. They were sayin', 'It's not the end of your life, you still got a long ways to go yet.' It was hard getting off that plane."

He managed a year-and-a-half stint with the Harlem Globetrotters, an episode that ended with a highly publicized drug bust in Brazil. After two more failed attempts at NBA rookie camps, Sam Drummer came home to Muncie in 1983 when his mother became ill. The hometown hero who had carried Muncie North to glory a few years before walked around town for two years looking for a job. He had no marketable skills and, apparently, few friends. Today Drummer works as a janitor at Ball State University. "I only got on out here," he says, "because this guy was startin' an industrial league and he said if I played he'd hire me." He is hoping to save enough money to join his girlfriend in California and buy a house.

Through it all, from high school to his current job, he has been known as someone who, as he puts it, "could jump outta the gym." Now thirty-two, Sam Drummer learned a lesson that many of the other 11,999 black high school players who fell off the ride, usually much earlier than he, could recite by heart: "I don't think they were interested in me as a person," says Sam Drummer. "Just as a ballplayer and nothin' else."

■

Each year, thousands of black kids like Sam Drummer jump aboard a powerful industrial belt, a separator, a jiggler and sifter and sorter that carries them, in progressively diminishing numbers, past recruiters and coaches and acolytes, into junior-college dorms out on the prairies, through meat-market camps in Georgia or Indiana. Like would-be Miss Nebraskas, they are measured, weighed, graded, tested, classified, inspected, and usually discarded within a decade. One serious injury ends the ride at once.

The first stop is the competition camp. Camps represent an enormous convenience for college coaches. Competition for prospects is so fierce, and the time to recruit personally so limited (the NCAA allows coaches only a span of about seven weeks during which they can recruit players personally), that coaches are willing to pay a fee for the chance to see a gymful of good high school players. The players, who receive embossed invitations announcing they are among America's elite, have to pay too. High school coaches explain to their players, especially marginal players, that if they want a future in basketball, they have to find the money somewhere, because recruiters have to see them play.

The B/C camp in Rensselaer, Indiana (there are also camps in Annapolis, Maryland, and Milledgeville, Georgia), has the air of a cattle show. Coaches pack the stands, clipboards glinting in the lights, and squint down at rosters bearing hundreds of names as numbered players shuttle in and out of several courts on the campus of St. Joseph's College. Each player, many of them from

America's poorest families, has sprung for over $200 just for the entry fee. Players also, somehow, have to pay for travel.

Camp literature makes it clear to the coaches that they are not allowed to recruit players during the camp sessions. The kids are forbidden fruit. Coaches, however mightily they may be tempted, however much their job depends on landing someone with serious hang time, are expected to get behind a door and grit their teeth and ride it out when the urge to speak to a prospect threatens to overcome them. Still, now and then, given human frailty, occasional indiscretions have occurred at basketball camps.

Al Harden, forty-seven, an ex–college basketball player and sports-shoe executive, remembers the experience of his eldest son, Rob, then a high school senior, at a summer basketball camp where contact with college coaches was forbidden. "[Rob] was approached by a counselor working there," Harden has recalled. "A high school coach. He said, 'Rob, an assistant coach from a top university is interested in you. He wants to know if you'll meet him on the grounds of the grocery store downtown.' Rob said, 'Sure.' I think this is a normal reaction from a sixteen-year-old kid who wants to play major college basketball.

"So picture the kid, pushing a grocery cart, not knowing who he's going to run into." The coach was waiting in an aisle. The coach told him he was just the white point guard they were looking for, that he could come and run their ball club for four years, that they would set him up in business after school. . . . Rob did not go to school there."

Bill Bolton, an ex–college coach and co-founder of the B/C camps says the camps are necessary, given the modern world of basketball. "How can anybody say it's not good?" he demanded in a 1985 interview. "Now, if you're just gonna go out and shoot on Sunday and say it's for the love of the game, fine, but I'll tell you what, it's a *business.* With the pressures on the pro game and the college game, if they wanna play and play right they need to be in a competition camp to develop their skills."

Many players go more than once, just as would-be attorneys take the LSATs several times. A bad camp, for a kid who can afford only one, can mean the end. "I went to B/C camp in Annapolis, Maryland," recalls Sherman Douglas, Syracuse University's All-American guard. "I didn't go in twelfth grade—I went in eleventh grade. I was playing with upperclassmen. In twelfth grade my game was better, and I'd have got more attention."

It was almost a fatal mistake. Douglas got tagged early as a sort of hybrid guard by the scouts who saw him play; it was said that he didn't handle the ball well enough to be what gets called, in the pseudoscientific babble of modern basketball, the one, or point—or lead—guard, or shoot well enough to play the two, or shooting guard. He scored like crazy, but in the wrong way.

College coaches who read about him in scouting reports saw him described as a young man with a serious taxonomic problem. "I tremendously underrated Sherman Douglas," concedes Tom Conchawski. "I rated him in the September 15, 1984, report, and I'm embarrassed to say, as a 'midmajor player.' Later on I upgraded him to a four plus. He didn't have much of a left hand. He wasn't a legitimate point guard. He didn't have a point guard's mentality. He was a penetrater, but it wasn't the kind of penetration where he had a great change-of-pace. He was sort of a 'slasher.' In my foggiest dreams, I never figured he'd be what he turned out to be."

But Douglas didn't know he was doing it wrong. To Sherman Douglas, the strange thing was that it didn't seem to matter to anyone that he was one of America's best high school players. As a senior, he led his high school to an undefeated season, the nation's number-two ranking and the D.C. city championship. He was named the D.C. Metro Player of the Year over Danny Ferry. He scored twenty-seven points a game. Not like a one. Not like a two. In fact, when he could, he didn't even wait around to play offense; he just stole the ball and laid it in. What he knew most of all was that none of the colleges he dreamed of seemed to care. At the end of his senior year he had one scholarship offer, from a place called Old Dominion University.

Sherman Douglas began to lose confidence. "I knew I had the ability to play," he recalls, "but it was always 'He was too small,' or 'His jump shot wasn't that good.' I was kinda skeptical about my skills. I had a little doubt about my ability."

One man, Syracuse assistant Wayne Morgan, acting on a tip from a D.C. coach, looked through the haze and saw Sherman Douglas. "And I *saw,* you know?" says Morgan. "No, he didn't play the point, he played the two guard. But every time they needed to score, or every time there was pressure, they gave him the ball.

"He didn't get to attend the Nike camp—he wasn't invited. He didn't go to any Five Star camps. He's a very poor young man. He couldn't afford the fees. He had been overlooked. People just said, 'Ahhh, five-ten, one-sixty-pound two guard.' But he had this *unbelievable* desire to compete. Every time he took the floor, he gave his heart and soul, and he expected the others to do the same. I could just see that, and I thought, With work, this kid could be good."

Morgan's offer of a Syracuse scholarship was the single chance for Sherman Douglas's dream of playing for a major college to come true. "I've been doin' this ten years and he was the easiest recruit I ever recruited," Morgan recalls. "I brought him to campus on a Friday. That Sunday morning I took him out to breakfast. I said, 'Whaddya think?' He said, 'I'm comin'.' "

Douglas, now one of America's outstanding guards, is asked one evening during a study break at Syracuse University what he would have done if it had all fallen through. "I'm really scared to answer that question," he says after a while. "I don't really want to think about not getting a scholarship to go to college. My heart was really set on going to college. To think what would have happened if I hadn't gone to college is just too scary. I don't know what would have happened."

■

For many, the second stop is a junior-college dormitory somewhere out on the range. Until recently, players who went to junior colleges were basketball's lepers. They were typecast as dumb, thuggish, morally defective kids who couldn't make it anywhere else. They were bastard children, vectors for failure who were rightfully quarantined in junior colleges so they couldn't contaminate the academic environment of the Big Eight or ACC (Atlantic Coast Conference).

But in August 1986 the NCAA passed what has become known as Proposition 48, an attempt to set minimum academic standards for athletic eligibility for freshman athletes at major schools. Proposition 48 requires incoming freshman to hold at least a C average in eleven hours of academic courses and achieve minimum standards on either the Scholastic Aptitude Test (SAT) or the American College Test (ACT).

Something had to be done. As of 1984, according to data prepared by the Center for the Study of Sport in Society, only 14 percent of all black college athletes graduated within four years, and 31 percent in six years. Those were about half the rates—in themselves dismal—for white athletes.

Basketball recruiters were panic-stricken. Now suddenly they not only had to find springy legs but had to go through the additional hoop of finding kids who could score a combined seven hundred points on the SATs. And it seemed unfair. Society had once again picked on athletes. Where were the incentives for nonathletes to prepare for college?

Just in time, recruiters remembered junior colleges. In a flash, the modest institutions that had been set up during the Depression or the Dust Bowl or with federal money so that local kids could go to school cheaply and near home became big-time basketball's halfway houses, stocked with urban academic underachievers who were suddenly viewed as rehabilitatable citizens.

A flood of high school prospects who failed to meet Proposition 48's requirements—most of them black—enrolled in junior colleges. According to the NCAA, 242 football and basketball players lost their eligibility in the first year under the proposition. More than 90 percent were black. Some major-college coaches were able to set up JC farm clubs, placing prospects with grateful junior-college coaches who promised to return them in two years—providing the coach still wanted them and the kid had managed to get an associate of arts degree.

In the second year, as Proposition 48 casualties began to pack the dormitories and lineups, subscriptions to Rick Ball's junior-college scouting magazine jumped from 2 major college subscribers to 125, including colleges that had failed to return calls for years. "I've had big-time schools say, 'Where have you been?'" says Ball. "I've been doing this for fifteen years."

Indiana University coach Bobby Knight, whose grudging willingness to recruit two junior-college players led to Indiana's 1987 NCAA championship, has been a special godsend for Ball. "Bobby Knight in one year made us all legitimate," he says. "Before that we had all been illegitimate. Coaches are like sheep. If Bobby Knight does it, it must be OK."

Maurice LaMar, now at Kankakee Community College in Illinois, is a product of Proposition 48. He grew up in an unexclusive part of Cincinnati, living with his mother and three brothers. He started out dreaming of Magic Johnson and Dr. J.—that is until later, when Michael Jordan began to push the envelope and redefine the notion of hang time. He blossomed as a senior, and became Cincinnati's co–Player of the Year. Like Sam Drummer, he studied just enough to play. "I knew I needed the grades to go to a big school, but . . . I don't know," LaMar recalls. "I was more worried about playin'. I just studied enough to stay eligible. I just coasted, like a lot of kids do."

His coach, John Grunkmeyer, says he tried to counsel LaMar to study more. "You can't believe how many times we talked about grades," Grunkmeyer says. "I'd say, 'If you study maybe you could go up to Dayton. You'll be on TV there fifteen or twenty times a year. You could be real well known there. When you get out, someone'll set you up in a business. You'll make thirty or thirty-five thousand dollars a year there and get a company car. The next person won't get the company car but you will, because you're a basketball player. God gave you the ability to do this. Don't waste it.' He'd say, 'Yeah, yeah.' "

LaMar first heard that he would have to take a college entrance test at the end of his junior year. He dropped by the counselor's office and leafed through a study guide, but he didn't take it seriously. "I didn't really prepare myself for it. I was guessing on a lot of the answers. The first time I took it I was gonna get a feel for what was on it for the next time. But the next time I didn't do as well as I thought I would have."

LaMar went to the B/C camp and did well enough to keep Grunkmeyer busy answering recruiters' calls. "Xavier. Wake Forest, plenty of others," recalls Grunkmeyer. "Then they'd ask about the grades and the ACT scores. I couldn't lie. I'd tell them his grades were about a one-six, but rising. They couldn't afford to spend a scholarship on a kid who couldn't play the first year. They'd say, 'Well, I'll check back.' "

So Grunkmeyer began to help LaMar choose a junior college. It seemed easy enough for a player of his caliber. But one April evening a small car in which LaMar and a companion were traveling left an Ohio highway at about a hundred miles an hour and struck a telephone pole. They had to cut LaMar out. Somehow, he survived with no permanent damage. The accident all but eliminated even the junior-college market and threatened his career until Grunkmeyer, calling in a chit with a coaching friend, was able to get LaMar a scholarship to Kankakee.

"Well, it's a start," LaMar said from his room in the Kankakee dormitory a year after the accident. "I got away from my friends, I can set aside some time for my studies. I'm taking English, algebra, psychology, and record keeping. I haven't decided on a major yet. Probably business." His life goal remains Division I, and then the NBA. It's what he's always wanted, and it's hard to look beyond that.

Maurice LaMar, a soft-spoken and precise young man, blames only himself for the becalmed nights along the Kankakee River. "I could have passed that [ACT] test," he says. "I really didn't prepare myself. The way I look at it I feel I made a mistake coming through high school. The junior-college route is a way of getting back something I should already have."

John Grunkmeyer, while agreeing quickly that LaMar could have and should have studied much more, feels maybe it's not that simple. "When I was a kid," says Grunkmeyer, who is white, "my mom used to have my clothes laid out and my lunch packed every day before school. Some of the black kids I've had are coming from situations so different. So much harder. I had one player who'd go a whole week without seeing his mother. She worked three to midnight. He did everything on his own.

"Everyone just wants to make the NBA. I try to explain the odds. *You* try it sometime. Magic Johnson. Dominique Wilkins. Michael Jordan . . . those suckers aren't real," says Grunkmeyer, his voice rising. "There's only three of them in the whole world."

■

Each year, forty or so fine pure nuggets sort out from the great mother lode of playground players and drop into the NBA. They have career expectancies of between three and four years; the one winner in twelve thousand claims the right to retire from basketball at twenty-six rather than twenty-two.

"What you try to tell them," says Tom Sanders, the former Boston Celtic forward and coach who manages the NBA's rookie-transition program, "is that, if they're lucky, they'll have forty or fifty more years to live after they quit. The things they do now can help those years. It's a helluva transition because they lose all their previous support systems. They're in a new city, they have money, new teammates, new coaches, and you have to prove yourself all over again."

Sanders brings in teams of NBA players, psychologists, and counselors to help with the shock of entry. "We talk about drugs and women and agents and all sorts of things," says Sanders. "Obviously they've become targets. These are people making a fair amount of money. About seventy-five percent of the kids are black, and many come from households that have not had that much experience with money. The kids won't have a real feel for it. And you get the expected result."

Sanders says that when he was a draftee trying to make the Boston Celtics back in 1960, he, like today's rookie, was concerned first and foremost about sticking with the team. But there's a difference. "We were targets in terms of fame, but not necessarily in terms of dollars. A rookie back then made seven to fifteen thousand dollars. There were many jobs coming out of school that made you that much. Now, the average salary in the

NBA is five hundred thousand dollars. The lowest they can make is seventy-five."

What, Tom Sanders is asked, would he say to the 11,999 kids who would do almost anything for the chance to be the one inside the gate, for a chance to receive counseling on how to handle predatory women, on how to cope with sudden wealth? "You don't take away dreams from people," Sanders answers. "You gotta go for your dreams. That's what life's about. If you had a kid who was playing violin and dreaming of playing Rachmaninoff's Chorale in B minor or whatever on a concert stage, hopefully you'd say, 'Keep working and practicing and hopefully you'll make it.' If a kid told you he or she wanted to be president, you wouldn't say, 'Nah, you're not good enough.' Encouragement, always encouragement.

"On the other hand, you would let him or her know that there are some realities. Like [LaMar's] car accident. Or an injury on the court. You'd try to give them some other options, so that if one doesn't work out, sure you'd feel the hurt, but you'd switch to the next track. Pressure them into other areas if it takes pressure. Because *you* know what's going on, you try to make them learn some other things."

Sam Drummer, on a break from his cleaning job at the Ball State dorm, answers without hesitation when he is asked what he would say to a kid, who, like him, wanted to grow up to play in the NBA. "I would say hit the books. Hit em' *hard.* Let the books be number one. Make sports be number two." Would he have listened to such advice as a kid? "Probably not," he says. "I wanted to be a pro."

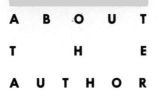

ABOUT THE AUTHOR

PHILLIP M. HOOSE is the author of two other books, *Hoosiers: The Fabulous Basketball Life of Indiana* and *Building an Ark,* about the conservation of endangered species. He lives with his family in Maine.